Candidate Support Provider Training

Participant Manual

© 2008 National Board for Professional Teaching Standards. All rights reserved. NBPTS, NBCT, National Board for Professional Teaching Standards, National Board Certified Teacher, National Board Certification are registered trademarks or service marks of the National Board for Professional Teaching Standards. Other marks are trademarks or registered trademarks of their respective organizations.

This project is funded in part with grants from the U.S. Department of Education and the National Science Foundation. Through September 2007, NBPTS has been appropriated federal funds of $167.7 million, of which $151.9 million was expended. Such amount represents approximately 32 percent of the National Board Certification project. Approximately $325.6 million (68 percent) of the project's cost was financed by non-federal sources.

Portions of the content of this publication were paid in part under a grant from the Department of Education. However, the contents of this publication do not necessarily represent the policy of the Department of Education, and you should not assume endorsement by the Federal government.

Acknowledgements

The National Board for Professional Teaching Standards® wishes to extend its gratitude and appreciation to **Joan Celestino (NBCT®, Winston-Salem, NC), Don Lourcey (NBCT, Statesville, NC), and Jill Saia (NBCT, Port Allen, LA)** for their time, energy, enthusiasm, and wisdom with the development of this new Candidate Support Provider Training. Throughout this project, these individuals provided content expertise on candidate support, contributed timely and meaningful feedback on all course materials, and delivered two pilot sessions of the new training in California. Without the dedication and expertise of Joan, Don, and Jill, the success of this training would not be possible.

In addition, the National Board wishes to acknowledge the contributions of the NBPTS® Faculty for their support and feedback throughout this development process, including:

Andre Audette, NBCT, West Greenwich, RI
Vickie Carson, NBCT, East Point, GA
Nancy Duggin, NBCT, Murfreesboro, TN
Terese Emry, NBCT, South Prairie, WA
Nancy Flanagan, NBCT, Howell, MI
Cyndi Herron, NBCT, Las Vegas, NV
Susan Hiles-Meadows, NBCT, Cincinnati, OH
Lynn Hines, NBCT, Bowling Green, KY
Heather Johnson, NBCT, Franklin Park, NJ
Leslee Milch, NBCT, Huntington Beach, CA
Carole Moyer, NBCT, Columbus, OH
Deanna Rogers, NBCT, Norcross, GA
Annette Romano, NBCT, Clifton Park, NY
Denecise Salters, NBCT, Blue Springs, MS
Kathy Schwalbe, NBCT, Goose Creek, SC
Jolynn Tarwater, NBCT, Potomac, MD

This training incorporates information from numerous resources, including NBPTS publications and other materials written by various authors. All outside sources of content are cited at the beginning of each module.

PREFACE

Welcome and thank you for participating in the NBPTS® Candidate Support Provider Training. We feel confident that you will find this dynamic program to be a challenging and worthwhile professional development experience.

While NBPTS values the diverse population of dedicated professionals who support candidates across the country, we also recognize that the quality and effectiveness of candidate support programs vary widely. We are also aware that while many candidates are being supported by individuals who are well informed and current on the National Board Certification® process, some candidates are negatively impacted by well-intended, but perhaps misinformed candidate support providers. Therefore, this training has been developed to bring accurate, current, and relevant information into the field and to foster greater consistency in how candidate support is delivered.

Developed by an experienced instructional designer with National Board Certified Teachers®, this training provides new and experienced candidate support providers with the practical knowledge, skills, and tools needed to successfully support candidates during the National Board Certification process. This training uses an active, participative approach to training where you will take part in a variety of activities to accomplish specific learning goals. We encourage and expect you to participate in all aspects of training including discussions, group activities, case-studies, and role plays.

This training offers answers to many frequently asked questions, clarifies common misconceptions about candidate support, and promotes best practices on a national level. Upon completion of this training, you will join a group of dedicated candidate support providers who provide consistent, high-quality support to candidates for National Board Certification.

Thank you for your commitment to accomplished teaching!

Note: This training is not open to current candidates for National Board Certification®.

TABLE OF CONTENTS

PRE-TRAINING SESSION: THE NATIONAL BOARD CERTIFICATION PROCESS

Session Overview i.2
Learning Objectives i.2

MODULE ONE: INTRODUCTION

Module Overview 1.2
Learning Objectives 1.2
Opening Activity: The Benefits of Candidate Support 1.7

MODULE TWO: THE FUNDAMENTALS OF CANDIDATE SUPPORT

Module Overview 2.2
Learning Objectives 2.2
Resources 2.2
Activity: Reflecting Upon Accomplished Teaching 2.7
Scope of Responsibilities of Candidate Support Providers 2.19
Activity: Different Types of Candidate Support 2.25

MODULE THREE: PROVIDING ETHICAL CANDIDATE SUPPORT

Module Overview 3.2
Learning Objectives 3.2
Activity: Reviewing NBPTS Guidelines for Ethical Candidate Support 3.5
NBPTS Guidelines for Ethical Candidate Support 3.6
NBPTS Certification Denial or Revocation Policy 3.14
Real-Life Scenario That Caused NBPTS Investigation 3.19
Real-Life Consequences of Misconduct 3.20
Activity: Reviewing Ethics Scenarios 3.22

MODULE FOUR: THE SCORING PROCESS

Module Overview 4.2
Learning Objectives 4.2
Resources 4.2
Activity: Providing Retake Support 4.15
The Retake Decision Process 4.19
Retake Worksheet 4.21

Table of Contents (Cont'd)

MODULE FIVE: WORKING EFFECTIVELY WITH CANDIDATES

Module Overview 5.2
Learning Objectives 5.2
Resources.. 5.2
Activity: Identifying and Overcoming Communication Barriers With Candidates 5.6
Questions That Push a Candidate's Analytical Thinking 5.11
Role Play Activity: Encouraging Reflective Thinking Through Questioning 5.14
Activity: Role Play Demonstration.. 5.22
Activity: Exploring Biases... 5.25
Activity: Recognizing and Resolving Situations of Bias 5.27

MODULE SIX: PORTFOLIO ENTRY REVIEW

Module Overview 6.2
Learning Objectives 6.2
Resources.. 6.2
Activity: What Is Descriptive, Analytical, and Reflective Thinking? 6.9
Activity: Identifying the Different Levels of Thinking... 6.12
Activity: Analyzing Portfolio Instructions 6.17
Sample Entry Review Note-Taking Chart 6.24
Cumulative Activity: Reviewing a Portfolio Entry 6.29

MODULE SEVEN: SUMMARY

Module Overview 7.2
Learning Objectives 7.2
Candidate Support Provider Training Course Evaluation Form 7.3

Pre-Training Session:
The National Board Certification Process

Pre-Training Session: The National Board Certification Process

Session Overview

The purpose of this session is to familiarize you with the National Board of Professional Teaching Standards (NBPTS) and its certification process. This session has been primarily designed for non-NBCTs who are working with or planning to work with candidates during the certification process. However, the content in this session can also serve as refresher information for individuals who have been through the certification process. **Therefore, anyone who wishes may attend this session.**

During this session, you will learn about the history of NBPTS, its core propositions and standards, and the assessment process for candidates. This session is intended to be delivered before the rest of the training modules, either the night before the first day of training or first thing in the morning of the first training day.

Learning Objectives

After completing this session you will be able to:

- Explain the history and mission of the National Board for Professional Teaching Standards (NBPTS).

- List the Five Core Propositions on which all NBPTS Standards and assessment activities are based.

- Describe the National Board Certification process including portfolio entry requirements, assessment center exercises, and the four stages of certification.

PRE-TRAINING SESSION: THE NATIONAL BOARD CERTIFICATION PROCESS

Welcome to the National Board Certification Process Pre-Training Session

Better Teaching, Better Learning, Better Schools

Pre-Training Session, Slide i.1

Notes:

Session Overview

This session has been designed for:

- Individuals who have never been through the National Board Certification process.

- Individuals who would like to be updated on the certification process.

Better Teaching, Better Learning, Better Schools

Pre-Training Session, Slide i.2

Notes:

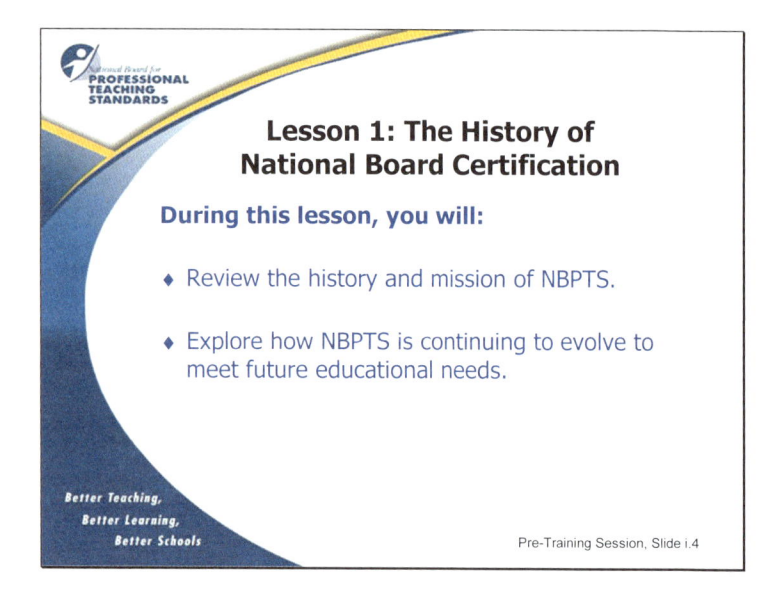

PRE-TRAINING SESSION: THE NATIONAL BOARD CERTIFICATION PROCESS

Session Objectives

After this session, you will be able to:

- Explain the history and mission of NBPTS.
- List the Five Core Propositions on which all NBPTS Standards and assessment activities are based.
- Describe the National Board Certification process.

Better Teaching, Better Learning, Better Schools

Pre-Training Session, Slide i.3

Notes:

Lesson 1: The History of National Board Certification

During this lesson, you will:

- Review the history and mission of NBPTS.
- Explore how NBPTS is continuing to evolve to meet future educational needs.

Better Teaching, Better Learning, Better Schools

Pre-Training Session, Slide i.4

Notes:

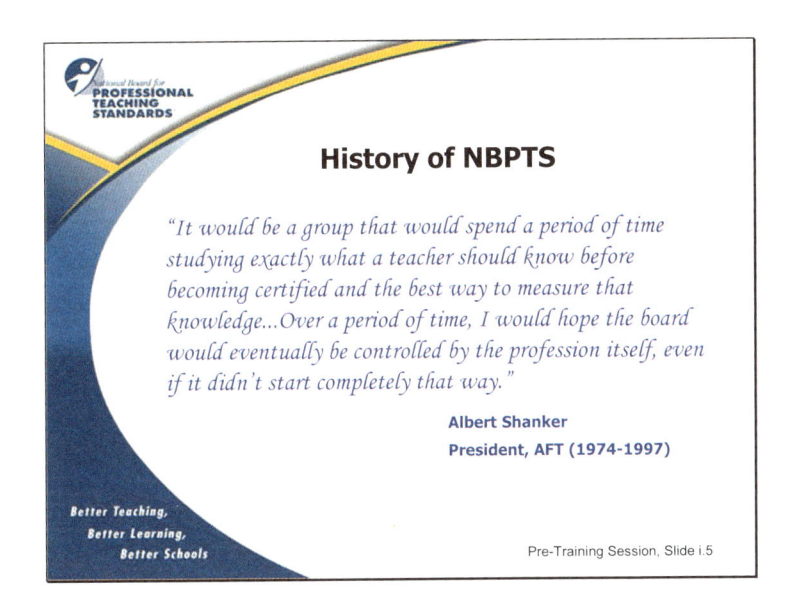

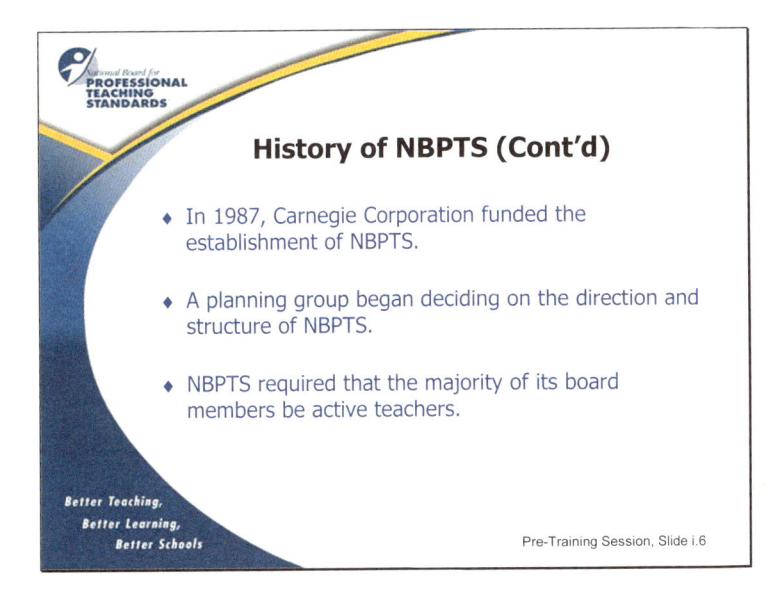

Pre-Training Session: The National Board Certification Process

History of NBPTS

"It would be a group that would spend a period of time studying exactly what a teacher should know before becoming certified and the best way to measure that knowledge…Over a period of time, I would hope the board would eventually be controlled by the profession itself, even if it didn't start completely that way."

Albert Shanker
President, AFT (1974-1997)

Pre-Training Session, Slide i.5

Notes:

History of NBPTS (Cont'd)

- In 1987, Carnegie Corporation funded the establishment of NBPTS.

- A planning group began deciding on the direction and structure of NBPTS.

- NBPTS required that the majority of its board members be active teachers.

Pre-Training Session, Slide i.6

Notes:

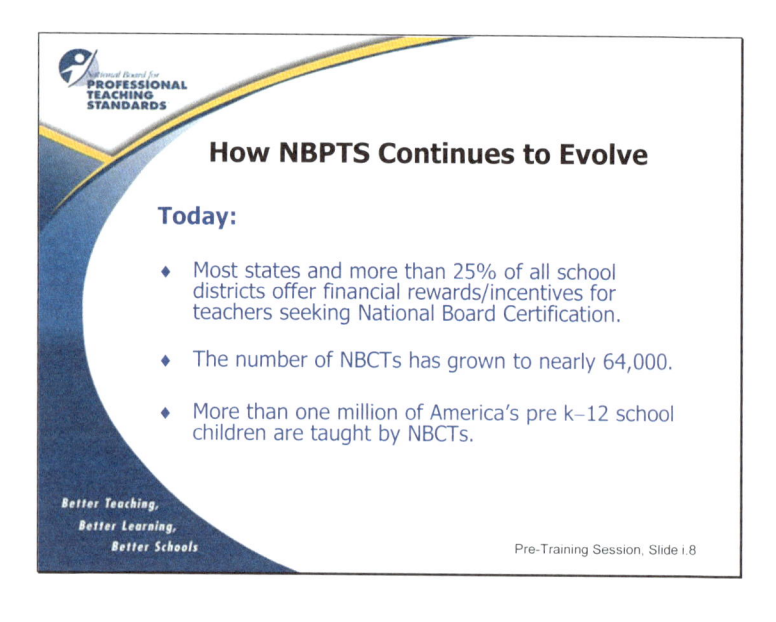

PRE-TRAINING SESSION: THE NATIONAL BOARD CERTIFICATION PROCESS

Mission of NBPTS

NBPTS advances the quality of teaching by:

- Maintaining high and rigorous standards for what accomplished teachers should know and be able to do.
- Providing a national, voluntary system for certifying teachers who meet these standards.
- Advocating related education reforms to integrate National Board Certification in American education.

Better Teaching, Better Learning, Better Schools

Pre-Training Session, Slide i.7

Notes:

How NBPTS Continues to Evolve

Today:

- Most states and more than 25% of all school districts offer financial rewards/incentives for teachers seeking National Board Certification.
- The number of NBCTs has grown to nearly 64,000.
- More than one million of America's pre k–12 school children are taught by NBCTs.

Better Teaching, Better Learning, Better Schools

Pre-Training Session, Slide i.8

Notes:

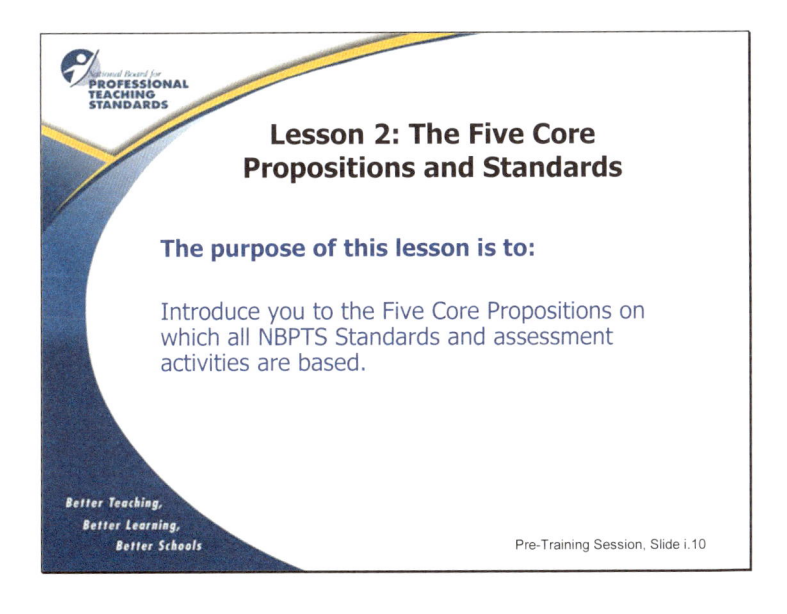

PRE-TRAINING SESSION: THE NATIONAL BOARD CERTIFICATION PROCESS

The National Board's Future Goals

- Expand the use of technology to simplify the certification process.
- Help define and support new roles for NBCTs.
- Continue to work with states to increase rewards of accomplished teaching.

Better Teaching, Better Learning, Better Schools

Pre-Training Session, Slide i.9

Notes:

Lesson 2: The Five Core Propositions and Standards

The purpose of this lesson is to:

Introduce you to the Five Core Propositions on which all NBPTS Standards and assessment activities are based.

Better Teaching, Better Learning, Better Schools

Pre-Training Session, Slide i.10

Notes:

Candidate Support Provider Training

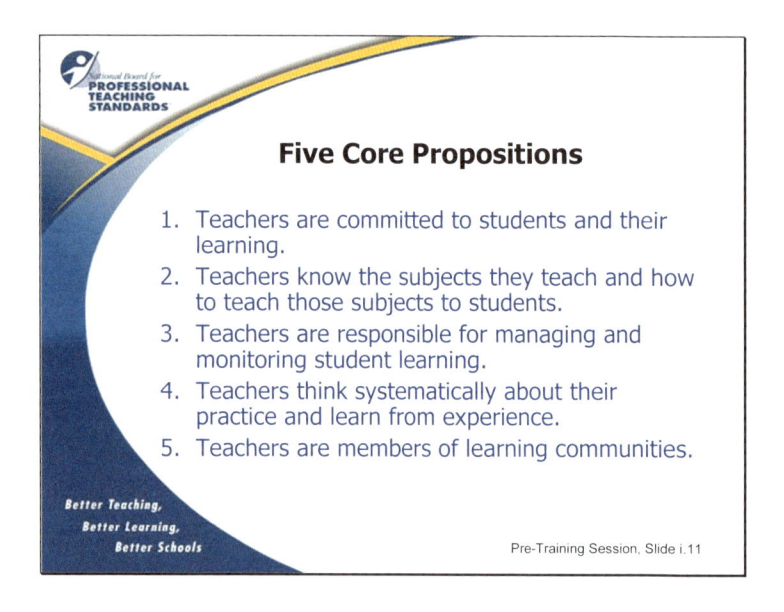

PRE-TRAINING SESSION: THE NATIONAL BOARD CERTIFICATION PROCESS

Five Core Propositions

1. Teachers are committed to students and their learning.
2. Teachers know the subjects they teach and how to teach those subjects to students.
3. Teachers are responsible for managing and monitoring student learning.
4. Teachers think systematically about their practice and learn from experience.
5. Teachers are members of learning communities.

Pre-Training Session, Slide i.11

Notes:

NBPTS Standards

- The Five Core Propositions guide the development of all NBPTS Standards.

- There are currently standards for 25 different certificate areas.

- Some standards common to all certificate areas are Knowledge of Subject Matter, Learning Environment, and Assessment.

Pre-Training Session, Slide i.12

Notes:

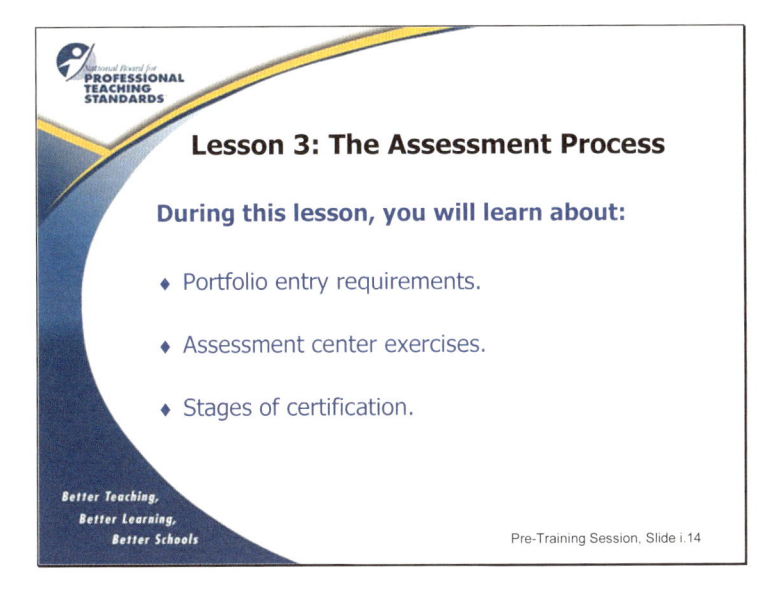

Pre-Training Session: The National Board Certification Process

Standards Development

- A standards committee is appointed by NBPTS for each certificate area.
- The committee provides recommendations to NBPTS about the specific standards for each certificate area.
- A draft of the standards is distributed for comment.
- The document is submitted to the NBPTS Board of Directors for adoption.
- NBPTS Standards committees are formed to periodically review the standards.

Pre-Training Session, Slide i.13

Notes:

Lesson 3: The Assessment Process

During this lesson, you will learn about:

- Portfolio entry requirements.
- Assessment center exercises.
- Stages of certification.

Pre-Training Session, Slide i.14

Notes:

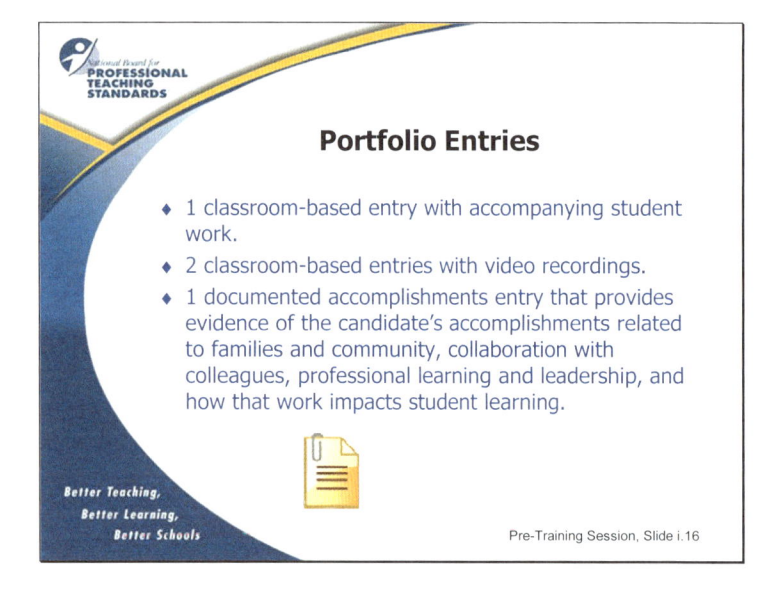

PRE-TRAINING SESSION: THE NATIONAL BOARD CERTIFICATION PROCESS

Overview of the Assessment Process

Candidates are required to complete:

- A portfolio of classroom practice.

- An assessment of content knowledge.

Pre-Training Session, Slide i.15

Notes:

Portfolio Entries

- 1 classroom-based entry with accompanying student work.
- 2 classroom-based entries with video recordings.
- 1 documented accomplishments entry that provides evidence of the candidate's accomplishments related to families and community, collaboration with colleagues, professional learning and leadership, and how that work impacts student learning.

Pre-Training Session, Slide i.16

Notes:

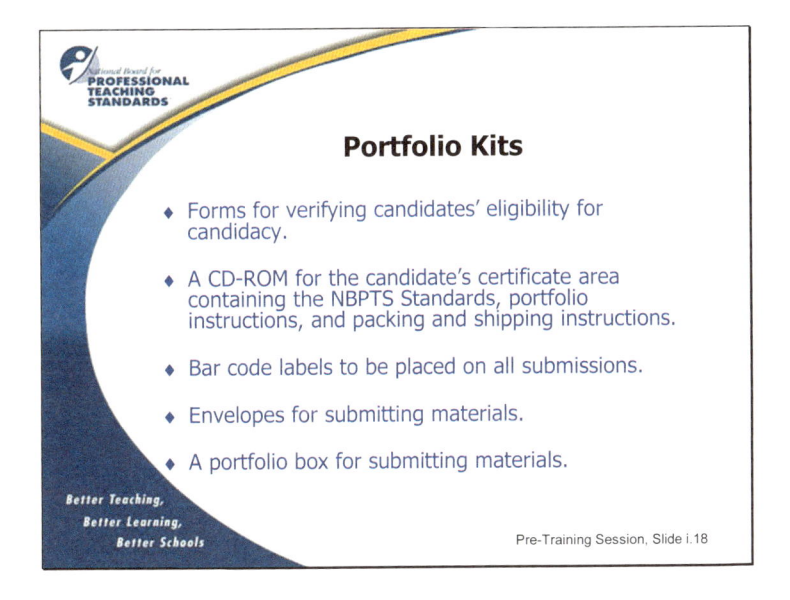

Pre-Training Session: The National Board Certification Process

Portfolio Entries

Each portfolio entry requires direct evidence of teaching or school counseling, as well as a written commentary describing, analyzing, and reflecting on this evidence.

Pre-Training Session, Slide i.17

Notes:

Portfolio Kits

- Forms for verifying candidates' eligibility for candidacy.
- A CD-ROM for the candidate's certificate area containing the NBPTS Standards, portfolio instructions, and packing and shipping instructions.
- Bar code labels to be placed on all submissions.
- Envelopes for submitting materials.
- A portfolio box for submitting materials.

Pre-Training Session, Slide i.18

Notes:

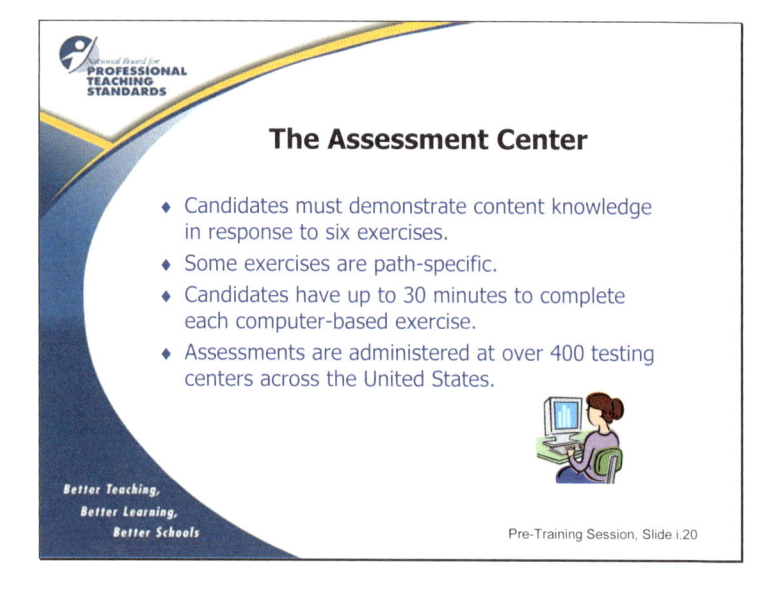

PRE-TRAINING SESSION: THE NATIONAL BOARD CERTIFICATION PROCESS

Portfolio Instructions

- The portfolio instructions are very lengthy and detailed.
- Encourage your candidates to begin studying them right away.
- Candidates can find them on the NBPTS Web site.

Pre-Training Session, Slide i.19

Notes:

The Assessment Center

- Candidates must demonstrate content knowledge in response to six exercises.
- Some exercises are path-specific.
- Candidates have up to 30 minutes to complete each computer-based exercise.
- Assessments are administered at over 400 testing centers across the United States.

Pre-Training Session, Slide i.20

Notes:

PRE-TRAINING SESSION: THE NATIONAL BOARD CERTIFICATION PROCESS

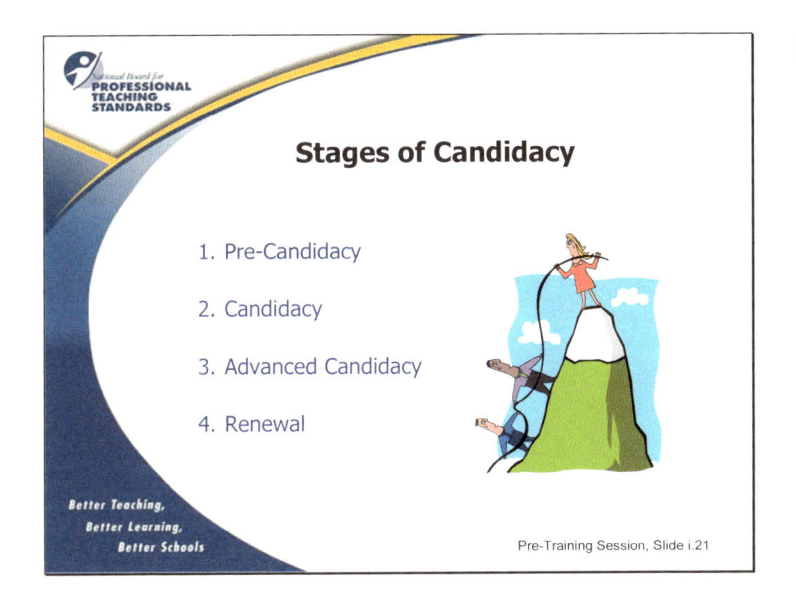

Stages of Candidacy

1. Pre-Candidacy
2. Candidacy
3. Advanced Candidacy
4. Renewal

Pre-Training Session, Slide i.21

Notes:

Session Summary

During this session, you learned about:

- The history of National Board Certification.
- The Five Core Propositions and standards.
- The assessment process.

Pre-Training Session, Slide i.22

Notes:

Candidate Support Provider Training

Module One:
Introduction

Module One: Introduction

Module Overview

This module is an overview of the training and provides you with an opportunity to begin discussing what it is like to be a candidate support provider. The module begins with instructor and participant introductions. Next, background information about the development of this training and an overview of the training is provided. The module ends with an activity that allows you to begin discussing the benefits of candidate support.

Learning Objectives

After completing this module you will be able to:

- Explain the purpose and goals of this training.
- Describe the new training materials.
- Identify the benefits of candidate support.

Module One: Introduction

Welcome to the NBPTS Candidate Support Provider Training

Better Teaching, Better Learning, Better Schools

Module 1, Slide 1.1

Notes:

Participant Introductions

Please provide:

- Your name.
- Where you are from.
- Your level of experience as a candidate support provider.
- Your certificate area.

Better Teaching, Better Learning, Better Schools

Module 1, Slide 1.2

Notes:

MODULE ONE: INTRODUCTION

Purpose of CSP Training

Provide new and experienced candidate support providers with the practical knowledge, skills, and tools needed to successfully support teacher candidates during their National Board Certification process.

Module 1, Slide 1.3

Notes:

Training Goals

- Explain the fundamentals of candidate support including its goals and benefits, the Architecture of Accomplished Teaching, and the roles and responsibilities of CSPs.

- Interpret and apply NBPTS guidelines that ensure ethical candidate support.

- Explain the processes used for scoring portfolio entries and assessment center exercises.

Module 1, Slide 1.4

Notes:

Module One: Introduction

Training Goals (Cont'd)

- Work effectively with candidates by applying adult learning principles, using effective communication skills, and putting biases aside.

- Review portfolio entries and be able to provide meaningful feedback to candidates.

Module 1, Slide 1.5

Notes:

Training Methods

This training includes:

- Presentations
- Group discussions
- Small group activities
- Individual activities
- Case studies
- Role plays

Module 1, Slide 1.6

Notes:

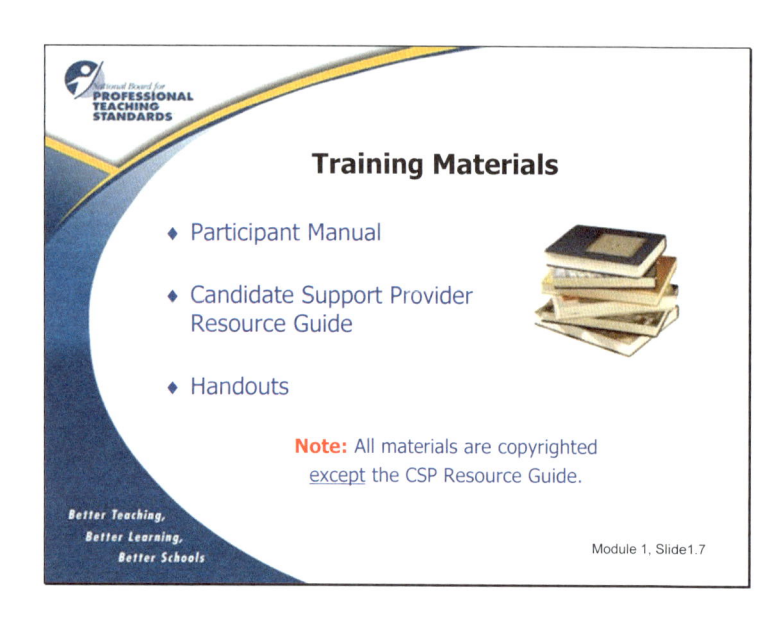

MODULE ONE: INTRODUCTION

Training Materials

- Participant Manual
- Candidate Support Provider Resource Guide
- Handouts

Note: All materials are copyrighted <u>except</u> the CSP Resource Guide.

Module 1, Slide 1.7

Notes:

Opening Activity

The Benefits of Candidate Support

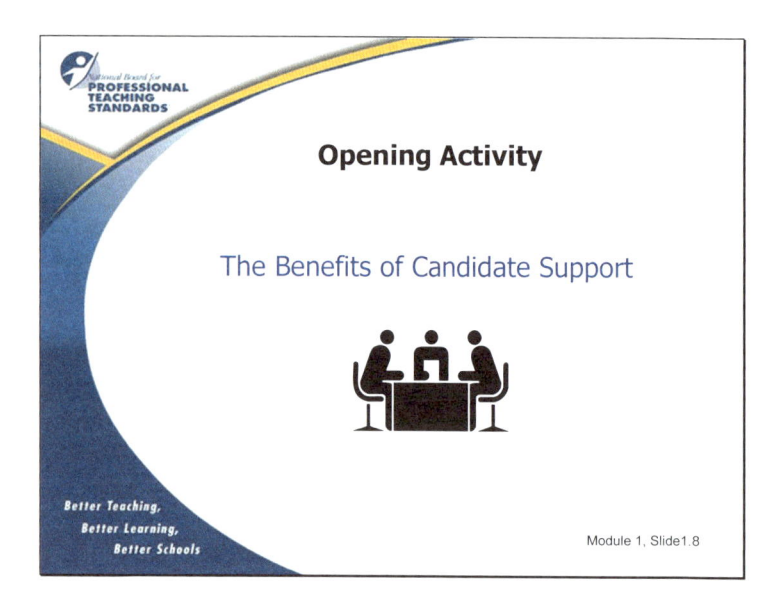

Module 1, Slide 1.8

Notes:

MODULE ONE: INTRODUCTION

OPENING ACTIVITY: THE BENEFITS OF CANDIDATE SUPPORT

PURPOSE:

The purpose of this activity is to brainstorm the wide range of benefits that candidate support provides.

INSTRUCTIONS:

From the questions listed below, work with your group members to brainstorm responses for your **one** assigned question.

- How do you think candidate support benefits **candidates**?
- How do you think candidate support benefits **CSPs**?
- How do you think candidate support benefits **students**?
- How do you think candidate support benefits the **teaching profession**?

Record your responses on your piece of chart paper. When you have finished, select a volunteer to present your responses to the class.

Take about **5 minutes** to complete your lists.

Module One Summary

During this module, you:

- Became acquainted with each other.
- Reviewed the purpose and goals of this training.
- Reviewed the training format and materials.
- Discussed the overall benefits of candidate support.

Module 1, Slide 1.9

Notes:

Module Two:
The Fundamentals of Candidate Support

Module Two: The Fundamentals of Candidate Support

Module Overview

During this module, you will learn about the overall goals and benefits of candidate support. You will review all components of the Architecture of Accomplished Teaching and learn how this structure forms the basis for the entire certification process.

You will also explore the roles and responsibilities of candidate support providers in the different candidacy stages. Another important skill you will learn during this module is how to set realistic boundaries with candidates and avoid helping too much or inappropriately. Finally, you will also be introduced to different types of candidate support that are provided including intellectual, logistical, emotional, and technological.

Learning Objectives

After completing this module you will be able to:

- Describe the goals and benefits of candidate support.
- Explain the Architecture of Accomplished Teaching and how the certification process is based on this structure.
- Describe the roles and responsibilities of candidate support providers.
- Describe the different types of available candidate support.

Resources

Some ideas and content in this module were adapted from the following resource:

Accomplished Teaching: The Key to National Board Certification, Bess A. Jennings and MaryAnn D. Joseph, Kendall/Hunt Publishing Company, 2004, pages 31-36 and 141-148.

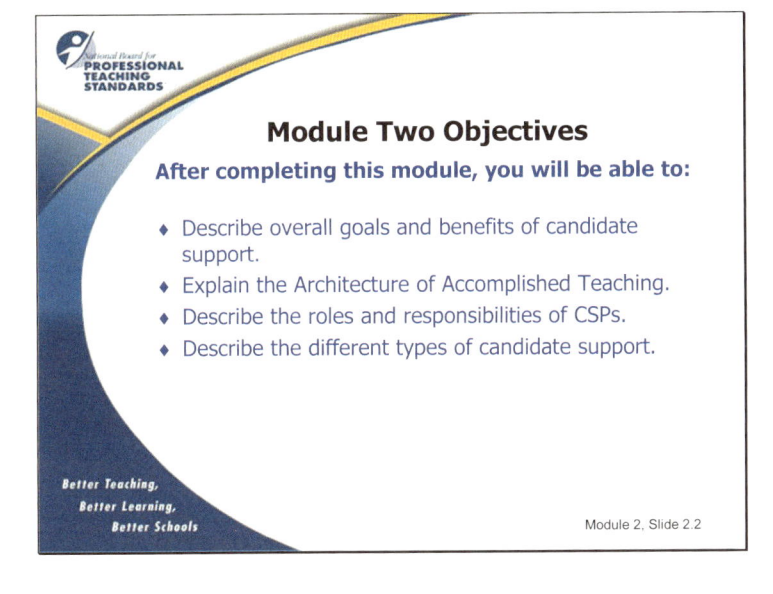

Module Two: The Fundamentals of Candidate Support

Module Two Overview

This module is divided into the following lessons:

- Lesson 1: An Introduction to Candidate Support
- Lesson 2: The Architecture of Accomplished Teaching
- Lesson 3: Roles and Responsibilities of Candidate Support Providers

Module 2, Slide 2.1

Notes:

Module Two Objectives

After completing this module, you will be able to:

- Describe overall goals and benefits of candidate support.
- Explain the Architecture of Accomplished Teaching.
- Describe the roles and responsibilities of CSPs.
- Describe the different types of candidate support.

Module 2, Slide 2.2

Notes:

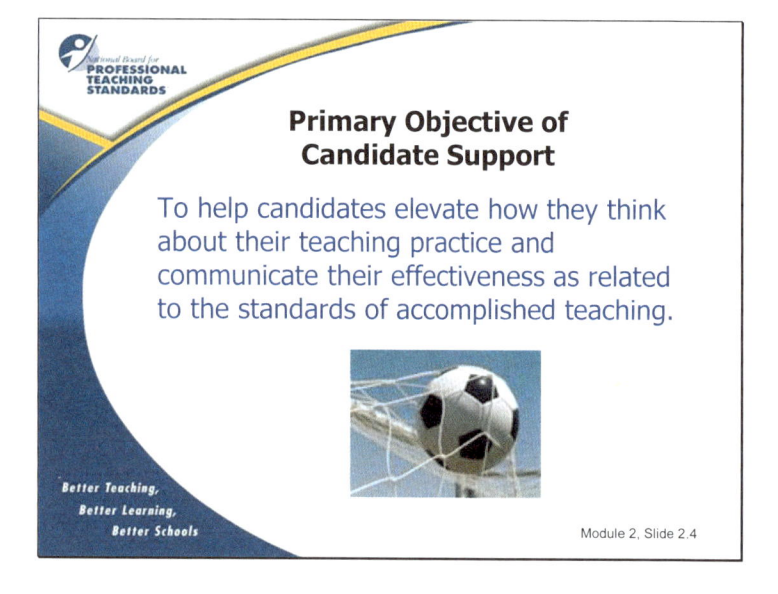

MODULE TWO: THE FUNDAMENTALS OF CANDIDATE SUPPORT

Lesson 1: Introduction to Candidate Support

During this lesson, we will:

- Explore the overall goals and benefits of candidate support.

- Review available resources for candidate support providers.

Better Teaching, Better Learning, Better Schools

Module 2, Slide 2.3

Notes:

Primary Objective of Candidate Support

To help candidates elevate how they think about their teaching practice and communicate their effectiveness as related to the standards of accomplished teaching.

Better Teaching, Better Learning, Better Schools

Module 2, Slide 2.4

Notes:

Module Two: The Fundamentals of Candidate Support

Secondary Objectives of Candidate Support

- Help candidates see the certification process as a professional development opportunity.
- Help candidates understand the standards.
- Help candidates understand the certification process.
- Help candidates reflect on their teaching practice.
- Promote candidate ownership of the process.
- Assist candidates with portfolio development.
- Prepare candidates for the assessment center.

Module 2, Slide 2.5

Notes:

Candidate Support Provider Resources

- 1-800-22TEACH®
- "Your Portfolio" box
- NBPTS Web site at www.nbpts.org
  - My Profile
  - Certificate Areas
  - The Portfolio
  - NBCTLink at www.nbctlink.org

Module 2, Slide 2.6

Notes:

MODULE TWO: THE FUNDAMENTALS OF CANDIDATE SUPPORT

Lesson 2: The Architecture of Accomplished Teaching

During this lesson, we will:

- Examine the Architecture of Accomplished Teaching.
- Discuss how CSPs can use this model when working with candidates.

Better Teaching, Better Learning, Better Schools

Module 2, Slide 2.7

Notes:

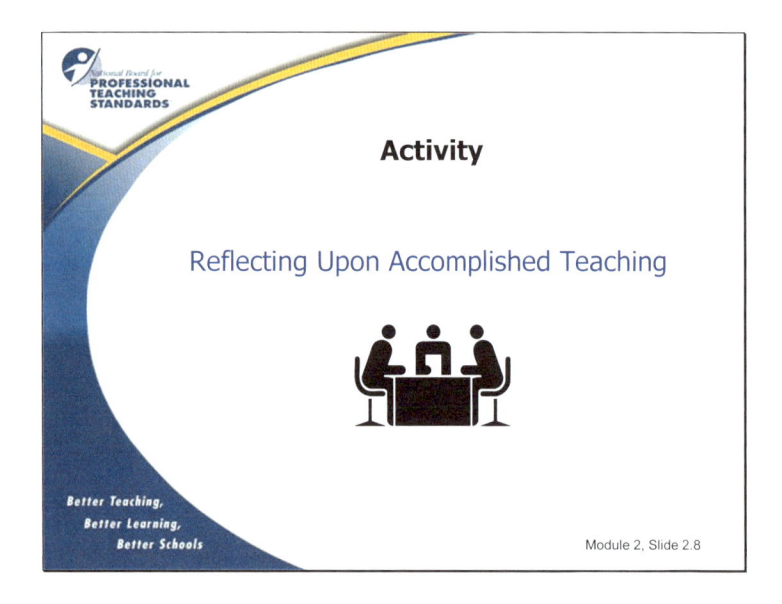

Activity

Reflecting Upon Accomplished Teaching

Better Teaching, Better Learning, Better Schools

Module 2, Slide 2.8

Notes:

Module Two: The Fundamentals of Candidate Support

ACTIVITY: REFLECTING UPON ACCOMPLISHED TEACHING

PURPOSE:

The purpose of this activity is to discuss what "accomplished" and "not yet accomplished" teaching looks like to you, based on your personal experiences.

INSTRUCTIONS:

Working in your groups, please answer your **one** assigned question from below.

- Imagine walking into the classroom of an **accomplished** teacher. What do you see and hear that tells you this teacher is accomplished?

- Imagine walking into the classroom of a teacher who is **not yet accomplished**. What do you see and hear that tells you this teacher is not yet accomplished?

Take about **5 minutes** to answer your question.

At the end of this lesson, we will revisit these questions and discuss responses.

MODULE TWO: THE FUNDAMENTALS OF CANDIDATE SUPPORT

NBPTS Five Core Propositions

1. Teachers are committed to students and their learning.
2. Teachers know the subjects they teach and how to teach those subjects to students.
3. Teachers are responsible for managing and monitoring student learning.
4. Teachers think systematically about their practice and learn from experience.
5. Teachers are members of learning communities.

Better Teaching, Better Learning, Better Schools

Module 2, Slide 2.9

Notes:

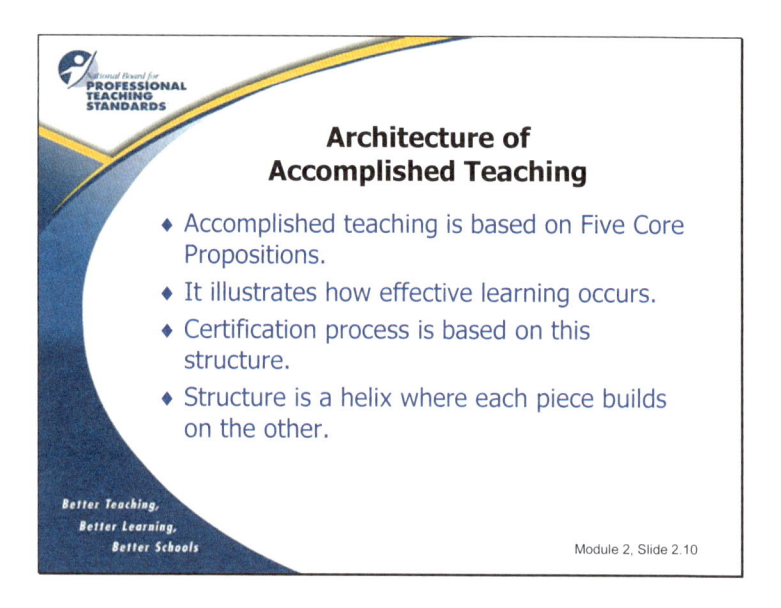

Architecture of Accomplished Teaching

- Accomplished teaching is based on Five Core Propositions.
- It illustrates how effective learning occurs.
- Certification process is based on this structure.
- Structure is a helix where each piece builds on the other.

Better Teaching, Better Learning, Better Schools

Module 2, Slide 2.10

Notes:

MODULE TWO: THE FUNDAMENTALS OF CANDIDATE SUPPORT

Architecture of Accomplished Teaching Helix

Your Students – Who are they? Where are they now? What do they need and in what order do they need it? Where should I begin? (1st)

Set high, worthwhile goals appropriate for these students, at this time, in this setting (2nd)

Implement instruction designed to attain those goals (3rd)

Evaluate student learning in light of the goals and the instruction (4th)

Reflect on student learning, the effectiveness of the instructional design, particular concerns, and issues (5th)

Set new high and worthwhile goals that are appropriate for these students at this time (6th)

Five Core Propositions

- Teachers are committed to students and their learning
- Teachers know the subjects they teach and how to teach those subjects to students
- Teachers are responsible for managing and monitoring student learning
- Teachers think systematically about their practice and learn from experience
- Teachers are members of learning communities

© 2005 NBPTS. All rights reserved.

MODULE TWO: THE FUNDAMENTALS OF CANDIDATE SUPPORT

Step 1: Know Students and Subject Area

The Architecture of Accomplished Teaching

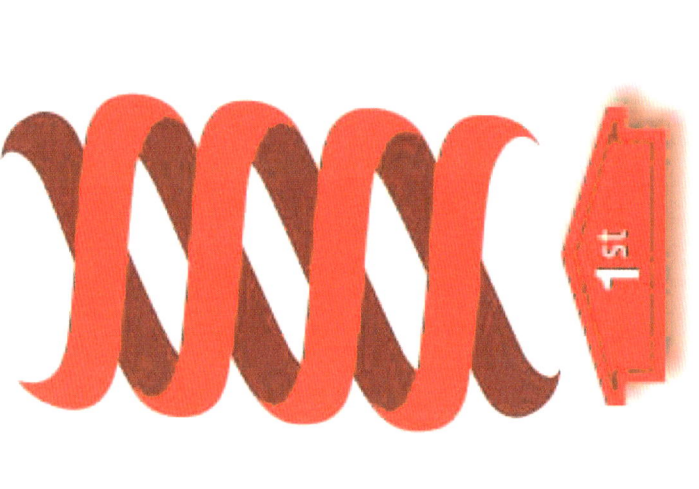

Step 1: Know Students and Subject Area
- Who are my students?
- Where are they now?
- What do they need?
- In what order do they need it?
- Where should I begin?

MODULE TWO: THE FUNDAMENTALS OF CANDIDATE SUPPORT

Step 2: Set Learning Goals
The Architecture of Accomplished Teaching

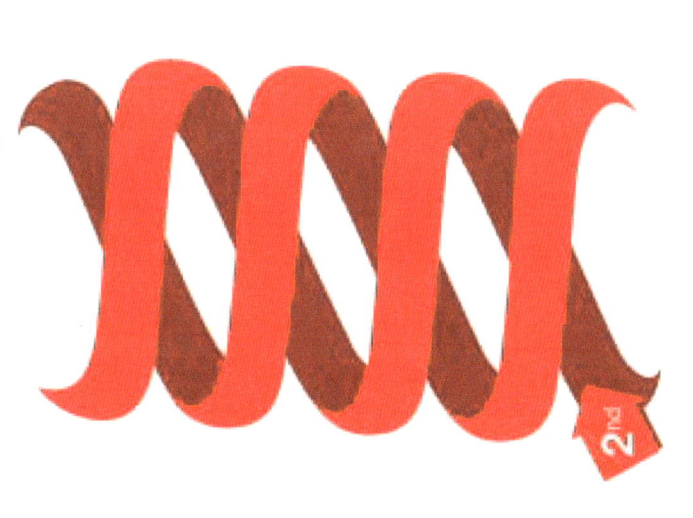

Step 1: Know Students and Subject Area

Step 2: Set Learning Goals
Set high, worthwhile goals appropriate for your students, at this time, in this setting.

MODULE TWO: THE FUNDAMENTALS OF CANDIDATE SUPPORT

Step 3: Implement Instruction to Achieve Goals

The Architecture of Accomplished Teaching

Step 3: Implement Instruction to Achieve Goals
- What instructional strategies would be most effective for meeting goals?
- What materials, people, or places can I use to enhance student learning?
- How can I vary the learning experiences and teaching strategies to meet the needs of learners?

Step 1: Know Students and Subject Area

Step 2: Set Learning Goals

Step 4: Evaluate Student Learning

The Architecture of Accomplished Teaching

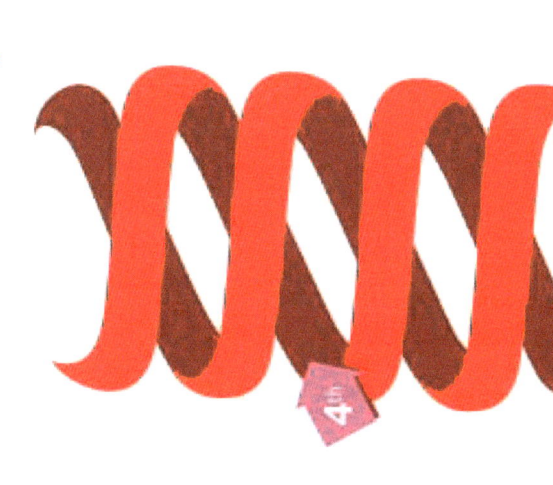

Step 1: Know Students and Subject Area

Step 2: Set Learning Goals

Step 3: Implement Instruction to Achieve Goals

Step 4: Evaluate Student Learning
Following instruction, evaluate student learning to see if goals were met.

MODULE TWO: THE FUNDAMENTALS OF CANDIDATE SUPPORT

Step 5: Reflect on Teaching Practice

The Architecture of Accomplished Teaching

Step 5: Reflect on Teaching Practice
- What would I do differently?
- What are my next steps?

Step 3: Implement Instruction to Achieve Goals

Step 1: Know Students and Subject Area

Step 2: Set Learning Goals

Step 4: Evaluate Student Learning

MODULE TWO: THE FUNDAMENTALS OF CANDIDATE SUPPORT

Step 6: Set New Learning Goals

The Architecture of Accomplished Teaching

Step 1: Know Students and Subject Area

Step 2: Set Learning Goals

Step 3: Implement Instruction to Achieve Goals

Step 4: Evaluate Student Learning

Step 5: Reflect on Teaching Practice

Step 6: Set New Learning Goals
Based on your evaluation of student learning, set appropriate goals for your students.

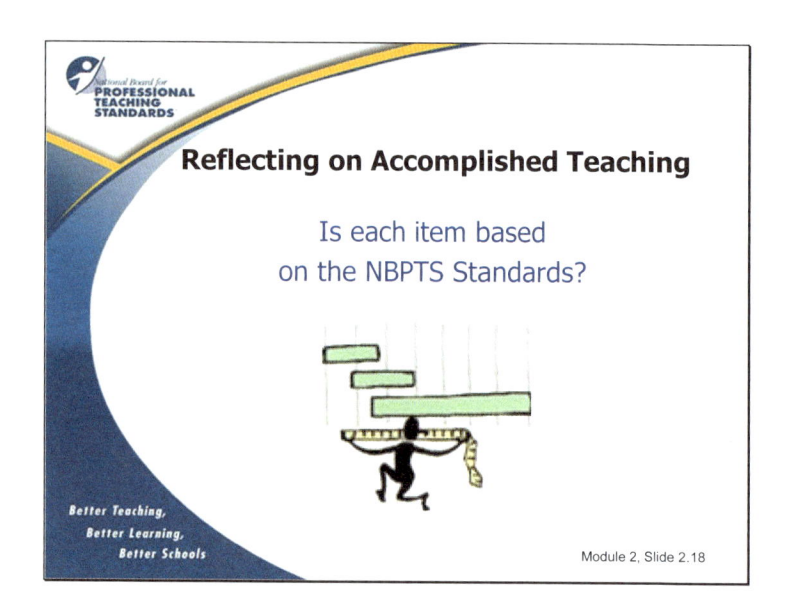

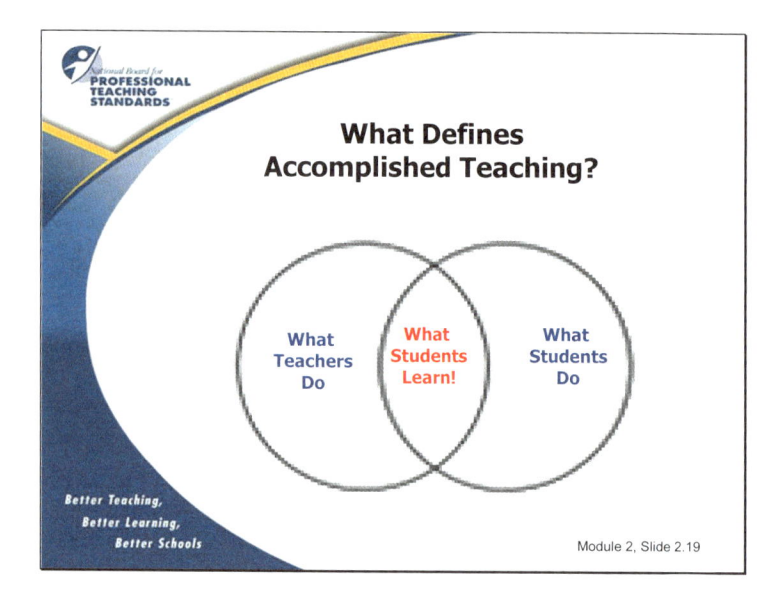

MODULE TWO: THE FUNDAMENTALS OF CANDIDATE SUPPORT

Reflecting on Accomplished Teaching

Is each item based on the NBPTS Standards?

Module 2, Slide 2.18

Notes:

What Defines Accomplished Teaching?

- What Teachers Do
- What Students Learn!
- What Students Do

Module 2, Slide 2.19

Notes:

2.16 NBPTS

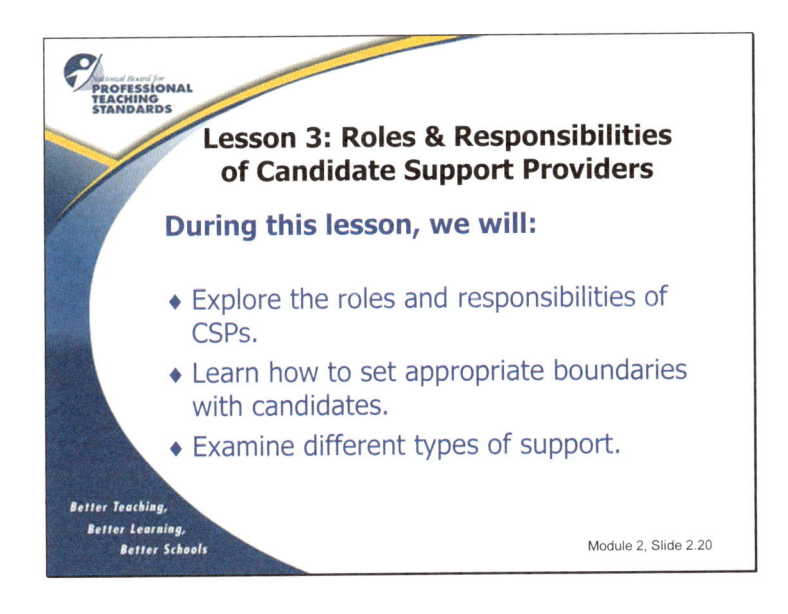

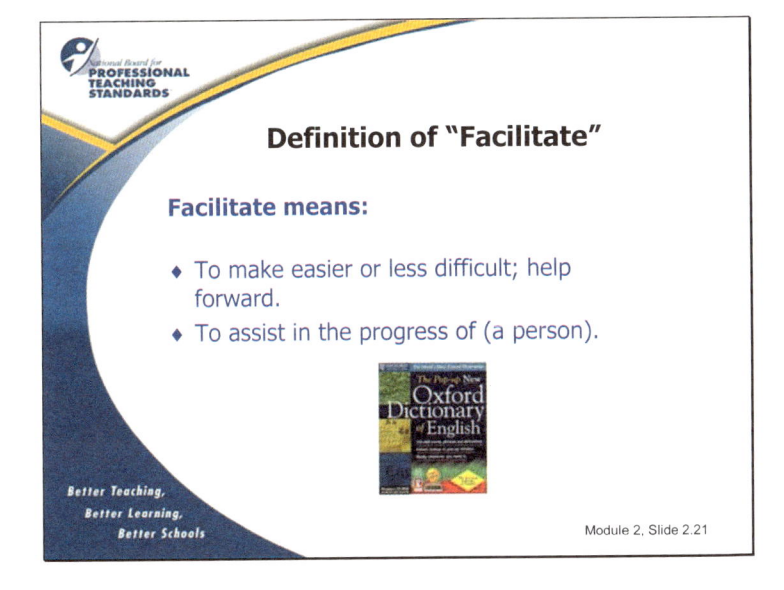

Module Two: The Fundamentals of Candidate Support

Lesson 3: Roles & Responsibilities of Candidate Support Providers

During this lesson, we will:

- Explore the roles and responsibilities of CSPs.
- Learn how to set appropriate boundaries with candidates.
- Examine different types of support.

Module 2, Slide 2.20

Notes:

Definition of "Facilitate"

Facilitate means:

- To make easier or less difficult; help forward.
- To assist in the progress of (a person).

Module 2, Slide 2.21

Notes:

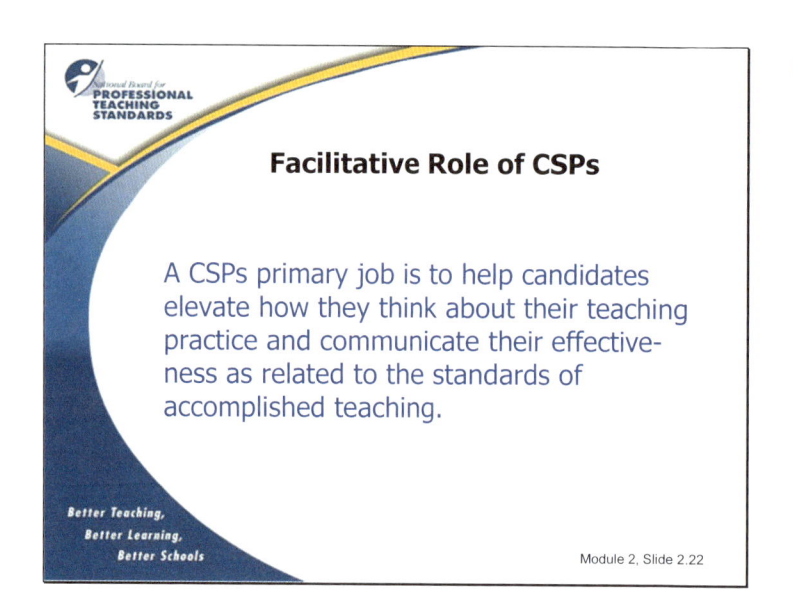

MODULE TWO: THE FUNDAMENTALS OF CANDIDATE SUPPORT

Facilitative Role of CSPs

A CSPs primary job is to help candidates elevate how they think about their teaching practice and communicate their effectiveness as related to the standards of accomplished teaching.

Module 2, Slide 2.22

Notes:

Scope of CSP Responsibilities

- Take One!
- Pre-Candidacy
- Candidacy
- Advanced Candidacy
- Renewal

Module 2, Slide 2.23

Notes:

Module Two: The Fundamentals of Candidate Support

SCOPE OF RESPONSIBILITIES OF CANDIDATE SUPPORT PROVIDERS

On the next few pages is a list of CSP responsibilities in the *Take One!*, pre-candidacy, candidacy, advanced candidacy, and renewal stages of the certification process. Review this list and add any additional responsibilities of your own.

Take One!

- √ Disseminate information about NBPTS and the certification process.
- √ Disseminate information about NBPTS and the certification process.
- √ Provide a clear understanding of the NBPTS standards and Five Core Propositions.
- √ Provide an overview of *Take One!* and the National Board Certification process.
- √ Explain how participating in *Take One!* can lead to National Board Certification.
- √ Explain the scoring process to participants.
- √ Ensure that potential participants are fully aware of the amount of work required to complete *Take One!*.
- √ Inform participants that they can download a given certificate's standards as well as the portfolio instructions from the NBPTS website before they receive their materials.
- √ Tell participants to read all relevant materials provided by NBPTS.
- √ Review the portfolio entry materials with the candidate, help establish timelines, and discuss procedural issues that need clarification.
- √ Establish a schedule for individual and/or group sessions to provide support for portfolio entry development.
- √ Help candidates understand how to provide clear, concise, and convincing evidence to document their own teaching practice in relation to the standards.
- √ Provide feedback to participants on their written work and videos to expand their thinking.
- √ Practice integrating the standards into the participant's teaching and writing.
- √ Provide encouragement and help ease anxiety throughout the process.

Other responsibilities:

SCOPE OF RESPONSIBILITIES OF
CANDIDATE SUPPORT PROVIDERS (cont'd)

Pre-Candidacy

- √ Disseminate information about NBPTS and the certification process.
- √ Recruit candidates.
- √ Assist candidates in determining if they are ready (i.e., knowledge, skills, and time) for the certification process.
- √ Guide potential candidates toward a clear understanding of the standards and Five Core Propositions of NBPTS.
- √ Explain what the certification process entails.

Other responsibilities:

Module Two: The Fundamentals of Candidate Support

SCOPE OF RESPONSIBILITIES OF CANDIDATE SUPPORT PROVIDERS (cont'd)

Candidacy

- √ Explain the certification process.
- √ Encourage candidates to begin reviewing and internalizing the Five Core Propositions and standards in their certification area. They can download the standards from the NBPTS Web site even before they receive their materials.
- √ Encourage candidates to commit to the project early and ensure that they are fully aware of the amount of work required to complete the entire assessment process.
- √ Tell candidates to read all relevant materials provided by NBPTS.
- √ Help candidates break the certification process down into manageable pieces and then complete each piece in a timely fashion.
- √ Encourage candidates to review portfolio materials even before they receive their "box" from the National Board.
- √ Preview the portfolio materials with the candidate, help establish timelines, and discuss procedural issues that need clarification.
- √ Establish a schedule for individual and/or group sessions to provide support for portfolio development.
- √ Help candidates understand how to provide clear, concise, and convincing evidence to document their own teaching practice in relation to the standards.
- √ Provide feedback to candidates on their written work and videos to expand their thinking.
- √ Practice integrating the standards into the candidate's teaching and writing.
- √ Encourage candidates to review and update content area information for the assessment center.
- √ Explain the scoring process to candidates.
- √ Make candidates aware of the NBPTS Guidelines for Ethical Candidate Support and the Certification or Denial Revocation Policy.
- √ Address questions about the certification process.
- √ Provide encouragement and help ease anxiety throughout the process.

Other responsibilities:

SCOPE OF RESPONSIBILITIES OF
CANDIDATE SUPPORT PROVIDERS (cont'd)

Advanced Candidacy

- √ Celebrate the completion of the NBPTS process before results are released, emphasizing the tremendous accomplishment of completion alone.
- √ In the few weeks before scores are announced, make contact with your candidate(s) to reassure them of your support whatever their results.
- √ Address feelings about the possibility of not certifying including denial, anger, and self-doubt.
- √ Explain how NBPTS banks scores.
- √ Assist candidates in determining which sections to retake if they didn't achieve the first time.

Other responsibilities:

Renewal

- √ Help candidates understand the renewal process including timelines and how it affects their status.
- √ Offer opportunities for professional conversation among NBCTs.
- √ Review and discuss any new and revised standards that have been written since initial certification.
- √ Discuss how the teacher has grown and developed since initial certification.

Other responsibilities:

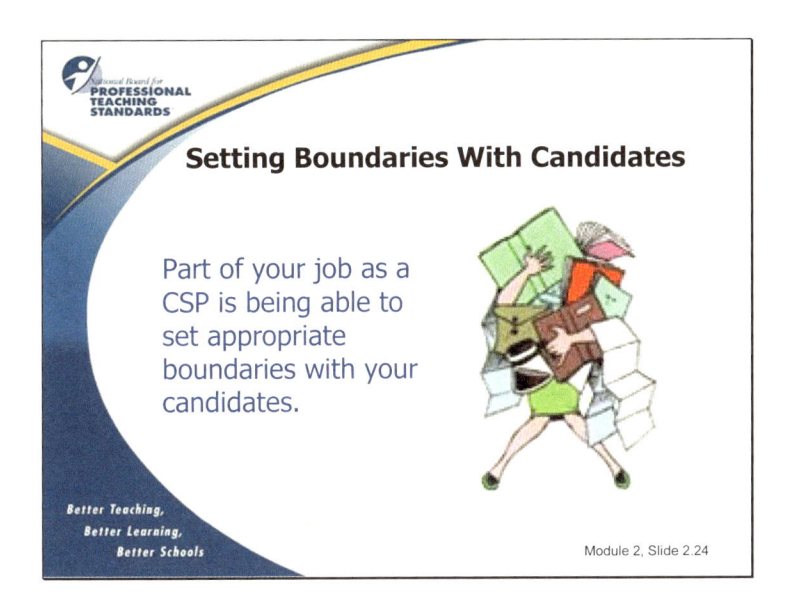

Module Two: The Fundamentals of Candidate Support

Setting Boundaries With Candidates

Part of your job as a CSP is being able to set appropriate boundaries with your candidates.

Module 2, Slide 2.24

Notes:

Guidelines for Setting Boundaries

- Don't share your portfolio.
- Avoid grading, judging, or scoring an entry.
- Resist emphasizing the way things used to be.
- Don't feel accountable for a candidate's success or failure.
- Resist making choices for candidates.
- Avoid the halo effect.
- Avoid overemphasizing the rules.

Module 2, Slide 2.25

Notes:

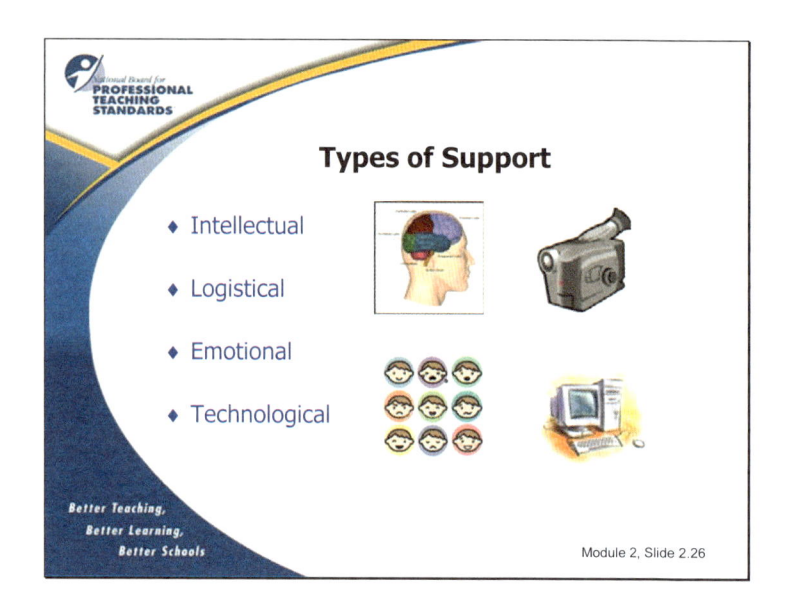

MODULE TWO: THE FUNDAMENTALS OF CANDIDATE SUPPORT

Types of Support

- Intellectual
- Logistical
- Emotional
- Technological

Module 2, Slide 2.26

Notes:

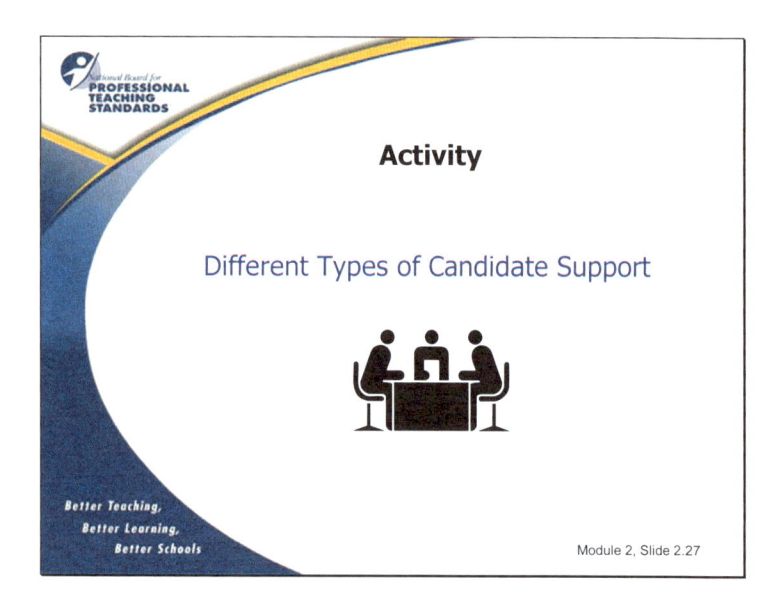

Activity

Different Types of Candidate Support

Module 2, Slide 2.27

Notes:

Module Two: The Fundamentals of Candidate Support

ACTIVITY: DIFFERENT TYPES OF CANDIDATE SUPPORT

PURPOSE:

The purpose of this activity is to brainstorm specific examples of intellectual, logistical, emotional, and technological support that CSPs provide.

INSTRUCTIONS:

Working with your group members, write examples of intellectual, logistical, emotional, or technological candidate support on your piece of chart paper.

Select a volunteer to share your examples with the class.

Take about **5 minutes** to prepare your lists.

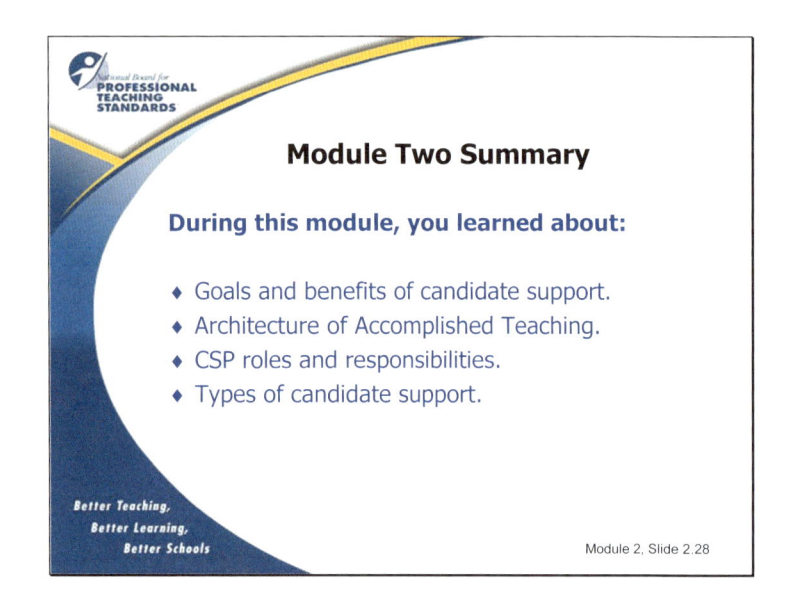

MODULE TWO: THE FUNDAMENTALS OF CANDIDATE SUPPORT

Module Two Summary

During this module, you learned about:

- Goals and benefits of candidate support.
- Architecture of Accomplished Teaching.
- CSP roles and responsibilities.
- Types of candidate support.

Notes:

MODULE THREE:
PROVIDING ETHICAL CANDIDATE SUPPORT

Module Three: Providing Ethical Candidate Support

Module Overview

During this module, you will have an opportunity to review and analyze the National Board's Guidelines for Ethical Candidate Support. You will also learn about the scope and seriousness of NBPTS' Certification Denial or Revocation Policy that applies to all candidates and CSPs. You will review real-life certification situations and determine if they represent ethical or unethical conduct and discuss why.

Learning Objectives

After completing this module you will be able to:

- Apply NBPTS Guidelines for Ethical Candidate Support when working with candidates during the certification process.

- Ensure that candidates fully understand NBPTS Guidelines for Ethical Candidate Support and Certification Denial and Revocation Policy.

- Differentiate between ethical and unethical candidate support.

Module Three: Providing Ethical Candidate Support

Module Three Overview

This module is divided into the following lessons:

- Lesson 1: NBPTS Guidelines for Ethical Candidate Support
- Lesson 2: NBPTS Certification Denial or Revocation Policy

Module 3, Slide 3.1

Notes:

Module Three Objectives

After completing this module, you will be able to:

- Apply NBPTS Guidelines for Ethical Candidate Support when working with candidates during the certification process.
- Ensure that candidates fully understand NBPTS Guidelines for Ethical Candidate Support and Certification Denial and Revocation Policy.
- Differentiate between ethical and unethical candidate support.

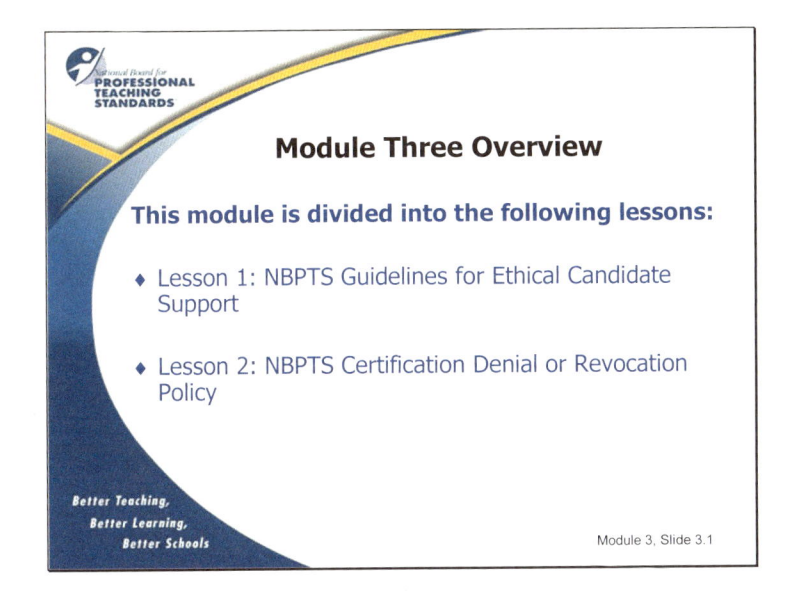

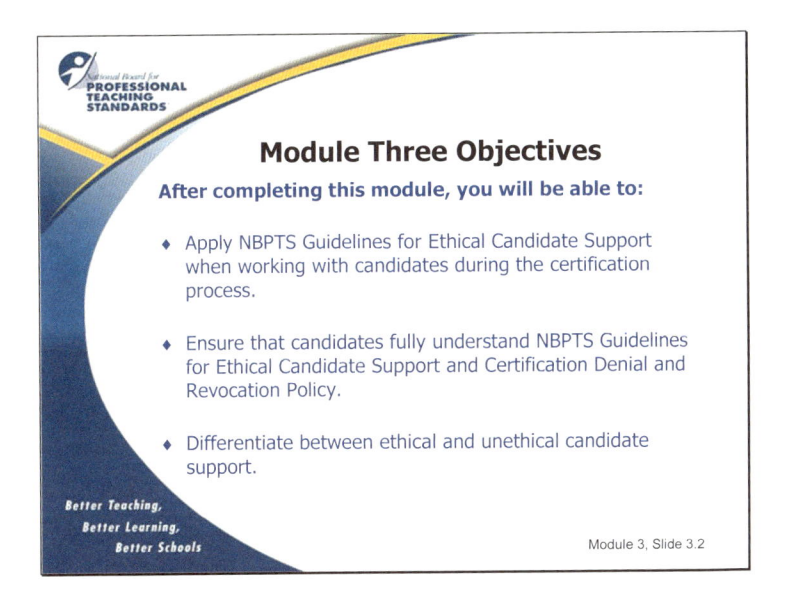

Module 3, Slide 3.2

Notes:

MODULE THREE: PROVIDING ETHICAL CANDIDATE SUPPORT

Lesson 1: NBPTS Guidelines for Ethical Candidate Support

- During this lesson, we will review and analyze the NBPTS Guidelines for Ethical Candidate Support.
- It is important for CSPs to understand and abide by the NBPTS ethics policy for candidate support.
- These guidelines were written as a safeguard for both candidates and CSPs.

Module 3, Slide 3.3

Notes:

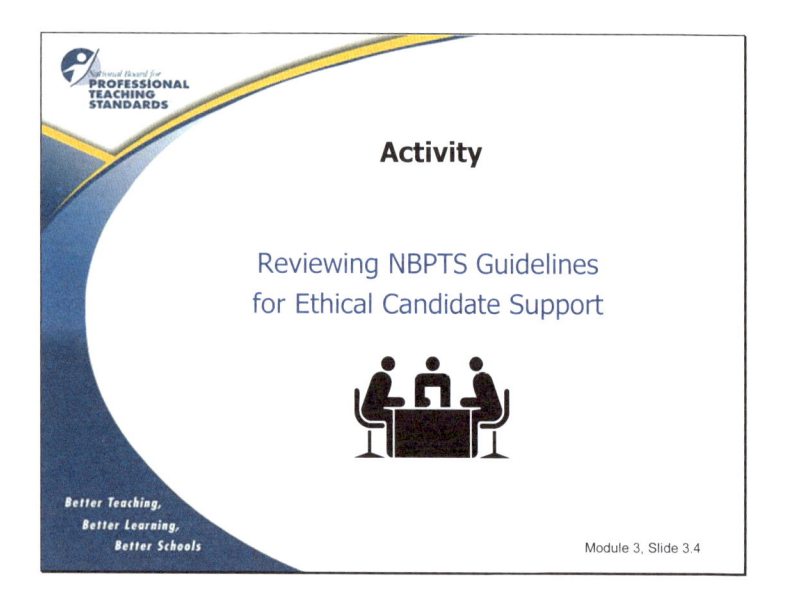

Activity

Reviewing NBPTS Guidelines for Ethical Candidate Support

Module 3, Slide 3.4

Notes:

MODULE THREE: PROVIDING ETHICAL CANDIDATE SUPPORT

ACTIVITY: REVIEWING NBPTS GUIDELINES FOR ETHICAL CANDIDATE SUPPORT

PURPOSE:

The purpose of this activity is to review and analyze the NBPTS Guidelines for Ethical Candidate Support.

INSTRUCTIONS:

Working individually, read the NBPTS Guidelines for Ethical Candidate Support on the following pages. As you read, underline or highlight sentences or phrases **and** words that you think are critical parts of this policy in guiding you as a candidate support provider. Be prepared to share your ideas with the class.

Take about **10 minutes** to read this policy.

NATIONAL BOARD FOR PROFESSIONAL TEACHING STANDARDS (NBPTS®) GUIDELINES FOR ETHICAL CANDIDATE SUPPORT

Candidates for National Board Certification® complete a rigorous process, requiring both intense self-analysis of their teaching practices and demonstration of their content expertise. Candidates consistently report that the process itself, independent of whether or not they actually achieve certification, is the best professional development they have experienced. Candidates also report that they benefit immensely from the support of a facilitator, or candidate support provider, during the certification process.

Candidate support includes providing resources, mentoring, coaching, guidance, and technical assistance to candidates. It incorporates intellectual, logistical, emotional, and technical support; however, the responsibility of developing and completing the certification materials always rests with the candidate. Candidate support may be offered individually or in groups, by individuals or through an organization, association, or institution of higher education. It can be formal or informal. Candidates may elect whether or not to participate in a candidate support program, and it is possible to achieve National Board Certification without participating in candidate support. However, teachers reported that candidate support, particularly when done in groups, kept them focused, motivated, and enhanced their understanding of their teaching practices and the decisions they make in the classroom. Good candidate support is nonjudgmental, honest, constructive, professional, and knowledgeable.

Candidate support providers are those individuals who facilitate candidates through the certification process, often starting before the teacher actually applies for certification. They may be National Board Certified Teachers (NBCTs), other accomplished teachers, staff developers, higher education faculty, or other persons concerned about improving education by making a commitment to work with candidates for National Board certification. Candidate support providers cannot make choices or create evidence for the candidate. Rather, the candidate support providers ask questions that help a candidate show evidence more clearly. Candidate support providers are sensitive to a candidate's emotional needs, help candidates create organizational systems to manage the process, locate resources to help with technology demands, and provide models of feedback that broaden and deepen the candidate's own analytical abilities. Candidate support providers have the opportunity to maximize the professional development experience of the national Board Certification process as they facilitate each candidate's journey towards documenting accomplished teaching. Thoughtful design and implementation of all aspects of candidate support create an intellectual and ethical environment that enhances the experience of teachers as they complete the process. This document provides guidelines to increase awareness of issues and actions relating to the ethical aspects of candidate support, to uphold the high integrity of NBPTS, to maintain the rigorous nature of National Board Certification, and to protect the secure processes of National Board assessments.

MODULE THREE: PROVIDING ETHICAL CANDIDATE SUPPORT

NATIONAL BOARD FOR PROFESSIONAL TEACHING STANDARDS (NBPTS®) GUIDELINES FOR ETHICAL CANDIDATE SUPPORT (cont'd)

Fundamental Responsibilities

Candidate support providers recognize that the National Board Certification process is voluntary and open to all teachers who meet the eligibility requirements defined by NBPTS. Accordingly, candidate support providers actively engage all teachers, including those in under-represented groups, in outreach, pre-candidate, and candidate support programs. Candidate support providers recognize the Five Core Propositions as the foundation for describing accomplished teaching. Candidate support providers acknowledge that the responsibility for developing NBPTS portfolio content and materials, and preparing for the assessment center, rests solely and completely with the candidate. Therefore, candidate support providers conduct support programs that honor and respect the professional choices and decisions made by candidates. NBPTS does not license individuals or groups providing support to candidates for National Board Certification but expects that candidate support providers ascribe to these guidelines for ethical candidate support. Candidate support providers manifest a deep commitment to the profession of teaching, NBPTS, the needs of teachers as candidates and pre-candidates, and, above all, students.

Commitment to the Teaching Profession

Candidate support providers believe that teaching is a profession, and they contribute to its growth by acknowledging that:

- Teaching is a public trust that requires adherence to the highest ideals of professional conduct;
- Teachers are lifelong learners who continually deepen their knowledge and skills; and
- Teachers keep current with research and information in their field.

NATIONAL BOARD FOR PROFESSIONAL TEACHING STANDARDS (NBPTS®) GUIDELINES FOR ETHICAL CANDIDATE SUPPORT (cont'd)

Commitment to NBPTS

Candidate support providers understand, incorporate, and act to uphold the policies and materials of NBPTS. Candidate support providers:

Policies

- Convey and uphold the mission, guidelines, and policies adopted by NBPTS, including all confidentiality agreements, the Certification Denial or Revocation Policy, the Policy for Use of NBPTS-Developed and/or Copyrighted Materials, the Policy for Use of NBCT and Veteran Candidate Assessment Performances (which includes portfolio content), the Policy for Use of Trademarks Held by NBPTS, and the Policy and Guidelines for Release of NBPTS Data for Educational Research;

- Understand that breaches of trust can destroy the validity of the certification process, notably that candidates cannot:

    1) falsify or fabricate evidence for any entries; 2) copy the work of other teachers or NBCTs to use in their own portfolios; 3) give, ask for, or receive information on secure assessment materials or information; or 4) share, publish, electronically post or otherwise reproduce secure assessment materials or information; and

- Share only information that is public for all candidates. Therefore, any individuals (including but not limited to staff members, consultants, scorers, and members of the board) with access to confidential information about NBPTS assessment exercises, scoring, or performance standards shall not reveal information or give the impression that they can determine whether a candidate will be or should have been successful in achieving certification or a particular score.

Actions

- Know and understand NBPTS Standards and the assessment process;
- Stay informed by using the NBPTS Web site, publications, research, and other resources to have the most up-to-date information;
- Maintain a clear distinction between personal opinions and NBPTS policies;
- Immediately report to NBPTS violations of confidentiality, incidents of falsified information or materials, or breaches of security at assessment centers by calling 1-800-22TEACH®; and
- Participate in NBPTS-sponsored training and use resources provided by NBPTS.

MODULE THREE: PROVIDING ETHICAL CANDIDATE SUPPORT

NATIONAL BOARD FOR PROFESSIONAL TEACHING STANDARDS (NBPTS®) GUIDELINES FOR ETHICAL CANDIDATE SUPPORT (cont'd)

Commitment to Teachers

Candidate support providers recognize their responsibilities to teachers (as pre-candidates, candidates, and NBCTs) in the design of programs and as they facilitate candidates. Candidate support providers:

- Acknowledge that there are multiple paths to certification;
- Understand that candidates alone are solely responsible for their certification materials and remind candidates of this;
- Conduct support in a manner that is nonjudgmental, honest, constructive, knowledgeable, and professional;
- Incorporate high expectations that encourage self-discovery and embody honesty, integrity, and trust; and
- Maintain agreements and commitments regarding the investment of time with the candidates they agree to facilitate.

Designing Programs

- Incorporate research and models of effective staff development and adult learning into programs and candidate support techniques;
- Design support programs that are equitable, maintain confidentiality, and are models of sound ethical practice; and
- Promote collaboration in professional learning communities as part of the professional development experience but emphasize individual responsibility and accountability in the development of candidate work.

NATIONAL BOARD FOR PROFESSIONAL TEACHING STANDARDS (NBPTS®) GUIDELINES FOR ETHICAL CANDIDATE SUPPORT (cont'd)

Facilitating Candidates

- Provide information about NBPTS in an equitable manner to all teachers and candidates;
- Direct candidates to specific NBPTS Standards documents throughout their certification process;
- Direct candidates to 1-800-22TEACH and www.nbpts.org as primary resources for candidate questions;
- Refer candidates to local resources including, but not limited to, university faculty, other NBCTs, and subject matter experts when appropriate;
- Demand honest and ethical behavior in candidates, reminding candidates of the agreements they signed upon application to the process;
- Provide support that is fair, objective, equitable, and respects confidentiality;
- Stress that all work submitted must be the candidate's own;
- Ask probing and/or clarifying questions;
- Encourage deep analysis and reflection based on evidence collected in the classroom;
- Do not hold their own submissions or teaching practice as models of correct practice;
- Give feedback, never estimated scores; and
- Help candidates find resources and comply with assessment procedures.

Resources

Guidelines for the following resources can be found at www.nbpts.org or by contacting NBPTS:

- Certification Denial or Revocation Policy
- Policies for Intellectual Property
- Policy for Use of NBPTS-Developed and/or Copyrighted Materials
- Policy for Use of NBCT and Veteran Candidate Assessment Performances (includes portfolio content)
- Policy for Use of Trademarks Held by NBPTS
- Policy and Guidelines for Release of NBPTS Data for Educational Research
- Programs designed to support individuals or groups as they proceed through the assessment process cannot be conducted by a member of the NBPTS Board of Directors or an NBPTS employee.

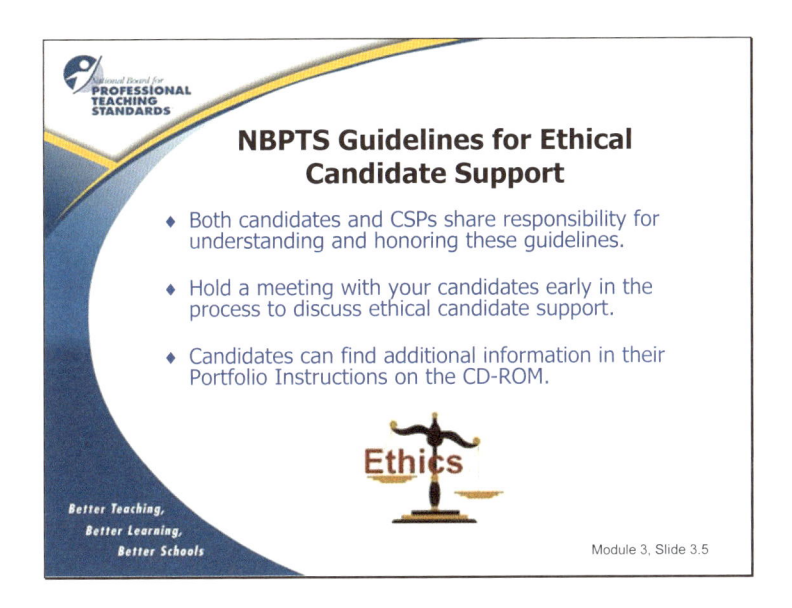

Module Three: Providing Ethical Candidate Support

Slide: NBPTS Guidelines for Ethical Candidate Support

- Both candidates and CSPs share responsibility for understanding and honoring these guidelines.
- Hold a meeting with your candidates early in the process to discuss ethical candidate support.
- Candidates can find additional information in their Portfolio Instructions on the CD-ROM.

Module 3, Slide 3.5

Notes:

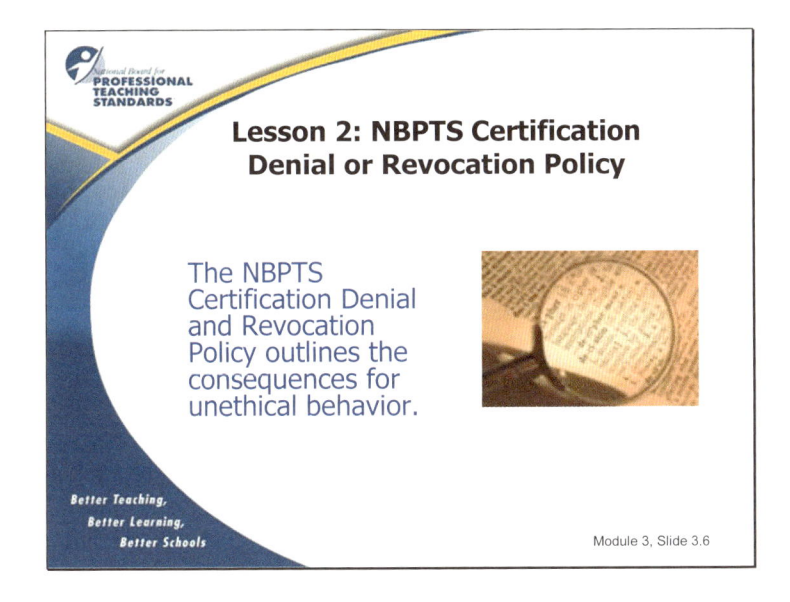

Slide: Lesson 2: NBPTS Certification Denial or Revocation Policy

The NBPTS Certification Denial and Revocation Policy outlines the consequences for unethical behavior.

Module 3, Slide 3.6

Notes:

Purpose of the Certification Denial or Revocation Policy

The purpose of this policy is to:

- Maintain the integrity of National Board Certification and prevent any candidate from gaining an unfair advantage over others.

- Allow the National Board to deny certification to a candidate or revoke certification of an NBCT for specified misconduct.

Module 3, Slide 3.7

Notes:

Consequences of Misconduct

The consequences of misconduct include:

- The release of names to the school principal, media, and district.

- Revocation of certification.

- Fines.

Module 3, Slide 3.8

Notes:

Module Three: Providing Ethical Candidate Support

Reporting Misconduct

- Call the NBPTS toll-free number 1-800-22TEACH®.
- You will need to share names before an investigation can take place.
- NBPTS takes swift action when misconduct is reported. Criminal investigations are launched and licenses are at risk.

Module 3, Slide 3.9

Notes:

NBPTS CERTIFICATION DENIAL OR REVOCATION POLICY

Adopted February 1995 -- Revised October 2002

The Certification Denial or Revocation Policy allows the National Board for Professional Teaching Standards (NBPTS) to deny certification to a candidate or to revoke certification of a teacher who holds a certificate as a National Board Certified Teacher for certain specified forms of misconduct. The Policy is intended to maintain the integrity of National Board Certification and to prevent any candidate from gaining an unfair advantage over others. This policy applies to all candidates for National Board Certification and to all teachers who hold a certificate as a National Board Certified Teacher.

I. Certification may be denied or revoked for any candidate or certificate-holder, who in the sole judgment of the National Board for Professional Teaching Standards,

   (A) Has knowingly misrepresented or falsified material information in connection with an application, credentials, assessment documentation, or other materials or information submitted to NBPTS, or

   (B) Has knowingly engaged in inappropriate conduct in connection with the certification process or renewal of the certification process, including, but not limited to:
   - (1) noncompliance with assessment procedures, regulations or instructions,
   - (2) violation of confidentiality agreements signed in accordance with the candidate application and/or assessment administration,
   - (3) obtaining improper access to secure assessment materials or information prior to the administration of the assessment,
   - (4) sharing, publishing, electronically posting or otherwise reproducing secure assessment materials or information,
   - (5) violation of the NBPTS guidelines that describe collaboration with others, or
   - (6) any other form of cheating or misconduct that compromises the integrity of the certification process.

NBPTS CERTIFICATION DENIAL OR REVOCATION POLICY (cont'd)

  (C) Has been convicted of a felony, has had a teaching license denied, suspended or revoked, or, in the case of an unlicensed teacher, has been fired or suspended, and where the conduct leading to such felony conviction, licensure action, or, in the case of an unlicensed teacher, firing or suspension, has involved:
    (1) Child abuse;
    (2) Job-related crimes;
    (3) Violent crimes against persons; or
    (4) Other conduct of similar severity NBPTS determines is inconsistent with the standards required of a National Board Certified Teacher.

II. NPBTS shall establish a fair procedure for such denials or revocations that is based on,

  (A) A finding by the President that certification should be denied or revoked based on the criteria in the preceding section and imposition of appropriate sanctions, including but not limited to:

    (1) Denial of certification and withholding of score report, with leave to retake one or more assessment exercise(s)
    (2) Denial of certification and exclusion from future participation in the assessment program
    (3) Revocation of certification
    (4) Assessment of monetary sanctions to cover costs and/or damages (including the costs of investigation) associated with the misconduct found.

  If the candidate or teacher does not request further review, pursuant to paragraph (B) immediately below, the findings and decision of the President will constitute the final judgment of NBPTS.

NBPTS CERTIFICATION DENIAL OR REVOCATION POLICY (cont'd)

(B) Upon submission by the candidate of a request for further review along with payment of the fee provided for below, a review of the evidence and issuance of a final decision, in its sole judgment, by the Disqualification Review Panel ("DRP").

    (1) The DRP shall consist of five (5) persons, who shall be appointed by the Chair of NBPTS with the approval of the Board of Directors, to serve for three-year terms. The Panel members shall be appointed from former members of the Board of Directors of NBPTS, and a majority of the Panel shall be persons who at the time they served on the Board of Directors were defined as regularly engaged in teaching elementary and secondary school students as defined by NBPTS. Any vacancies on the Panel may be filled by appointments by the Chair of NBPTS Board of Directors to serve the remaining term. No Panel member may serve more than two consecutive three-year terms.

        (a) Voluntary Resignation. Any member of the Disqualification Review Panel may resign at any time by notifying the Chair or the Secretary in writing. Such resignation shall take effect at the time specified by the resigning member, or, if no time is specified, on receipt by the Chair or the Secretary of the notice of resignation.

        (b) Mandatory Tender of Notice and Resignation. In order to assure that a majority of the Disqualification Review Panel shall be persons who are regularly engaged in teaching elementary and secondary school children, any person elected to the panel in this class who ceases such teaching for any reason shall so notify the Chair or the Secretary in writing. Unless the change from the teaching status is limited by its terms to one year or less, the member shall also tender her or his resignation, effective immediately to the Chair or the Secretary. The Chair and/or Secretary shall report to the Board of Directors all such mandatory tendered notices and resignations.

        (c) Of those five members of the Disqualification Review Panel, one shall be assigned by lot to a one-year term, two shall be assigned by lot to two-year terms, and the other two shall be assigned to three-year terms.

MODULE THREE: PROVIDING ETHICAL CANDIDATE SUPPORT

NBPTS CERTIFICATION DENIAL OR REVOCATION POLICY (cont'd)

(2) It is preferred that all five members be presented for the DRP to take action. Action by the DRP requires a quorum of three members and shall be by majority vote. A member of the DRP may elect not to participate in one or more decisions of the panel for any reason, and shall elect not to participate in any decision where the member determines, in his or her sole discretion; he or she for any reason is not able to act fairly and impartially. If one or more members of the DRP cannot participate, the Chair of NBPTS shall appoint a person qualified to serve on the DRP. The DRP may meet in person or by telephone. The decision of the DRP shall constitute the final judgment of NBPTS

III. In the interest of public protection and protecting the integrity of the teaching profession, for all teachers who have been denied certification and excluded from future participation in the assessment program or had a National Board Certificate revoked, NBPTS will:

(A) Provide the following information to the agency responsible for state licensure, employers, as well as to any third-party payer who financially supported or supports the teacher involved:
   (1) Teacher name
   (2) Teacher home address, city and state
   (3) Teacher school
   (4) Date of action taken by NBPTS

(B) Remove the name of the teacher from any NBPTS official listing of National Board Certified Teachers

(C) Make the following information available through online and print publications and press releases:
   (1) Teacher name
   (2) Teacher city and state
   (3) Date of action taken by NBPTS

NBPTS CERTIFICATION DENIAL OR REVOCATION POLICY (cont'd)

IV. NBPTS shall establish a filing fee or charge that will be assessed to and must be paid by teachers who seek review of the President's finding under this policy. The amount of that filing fee or charge is set by the President of NBPTS, who may alter or revise the amount of that fee or charge from time to time.

V. The President shall regularly submit a report to the Board of Directors on the implementation of this policy.

MODULE THREE: PROVIDING ETHICAL CANDIDATE SUPPORT

REAL-LIFE SCENARIO THAT CAUSED NBPTS INVESTIGATION

SCENARIO

An NBCT candidate support provider regularly met with six first-time candidates pursuing National Board Certification. The group met at the NBCT's home every Monday night. All six candidates were pursuing certification in the same certificate field.

One of the six candidates made his assessment center appointment for a particular Saturday. The appointments for the remaining five candidates were scheduled on the following Saturday. The NBCT candidate support provider asked the first candidate to memorize the prompts so that he could share them with his five colleagues during their Monday evening candidate support meeting. That way, the NBCT suggested, the candidate's colleagues would be assured of being successful. This would not only help all of her candidates, the NBCT believed, but would also meet the NBCT's goal of achieving a 100% success rate among those for whom she provided candidate support.

As requested by the NBCT, the candidate shared all six assessment center prompts with his colleagues on the Monday evening following his Saturday appointment.

MODULE THREE: PROVIDING ETHICAL CANDIDATE SUPPORT

REAL-LIFE CONSEQUENCES OF MISCONDUCT

CONSEQUENCES

A test security investigation team which included former law enforcement officers, was dispatched to the location to conduct an investigation, including personal interviews in the homes of all those involved. The NBCT's certificate was placed before the NBPTS Disqualification Review Panel for consideration of revocation in accordance with the NBPTS Certification Denial or Revocation Policy.

The candidates involved faced possible denial of certification and/or permanent disqualification by the NBPTS Disqualification Review Panel. NBPTS temporarily halted all testing in that certificate field to discard and replace the exposed prompts, creating inconvenience for other candidates whose appointments were delayed. NBPTS incurred a significant expense in the loss of six prompts and the development of their replacements.

The state wished to conduct its own investigation, since some of individuals involved in the incident had received state funds in payment of candidate fees — thereby making this a criminal case due to the fraudulent use of state funds.

Note: Scenario materials taken from NBPTS archives.

Module Three: Providing Ethical Candidate Support

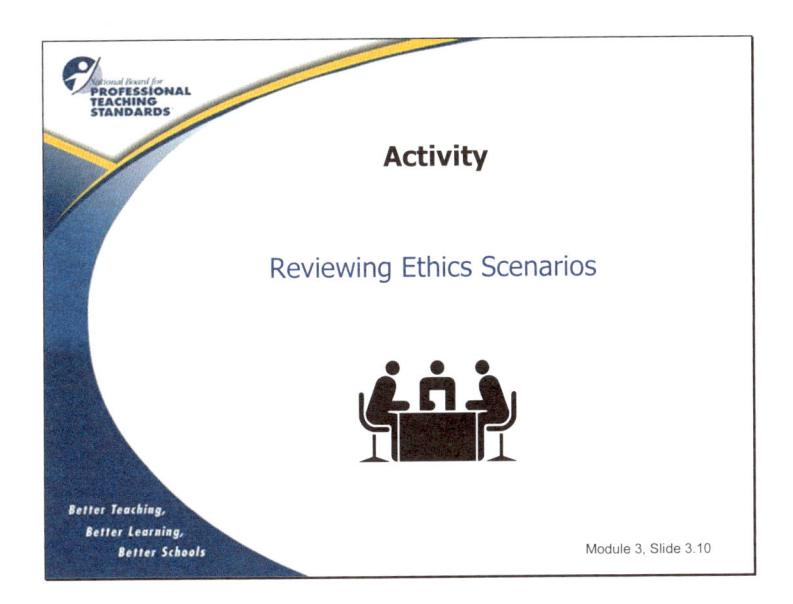

Activity

Reviewing Ethics Scenarios

Module 3, Slide 3.10

Notes:

MODULE THREE: PROVIDING ETHICAL CANDIDATE SUPPORT

ACTIVITY: REVIEWING ETHICS SCENARIOS

PURPOSE:

The purpose of this activity is to examine and discuss real-life candidate support situations that deal with ethical issues.

INSTRUCTIONS:

Review your assigned scenario on the following pages. Working as a group, determine if the situation is ethical or unethical and explain why. Select a spokesperson to present your results to the class.

Take about **5 minutes** to read and discuss this scenario.

MODULE THREE: PROVIDING ETHICAL CANDIDATE SUPPORT

ACTIVITY: REVIEWING ETHICS SCENARIOS (cont'd)

SCENARIO #1

A widely respected education professor with 30 years of experience in reading and responding to the work of graduate students in education becomes interested in National Board Certification. He offers to read the work of candidates in his state — a state that has no formal candidate support system. He reads their entries and grades them. Several of the candidates who have been given A "grades" on their entries do not certify. They are convinced that the assessment process does not identify accomplished teaching.

Is this situation ethical or unethical? Why?

Note: Scenario materials provided and adapted by Nancy Flanagan, NBCT.

MODULE THREE: PROVIDING ETHICAL CANDIDATE SUPPORT

ACTIVITY: REVIEWING ETHICS SCENARIOS (cont'd)

SCENARIO #2

An experienced candidate support provider (who is receiving a state stipend) tells all her candidates that they must italicize the questions in the portfolio directions and include them in their entries. She tells them she did this and certified " …with points to spare…" She also tells them she doesn't know a single NBCT who didn't include the questions in the portfolio entries, and that assessors are trained to follow the questions in their scoring.

Is this situation ethical or unethical? Why?

Note: Scenario materials provided and adapted by Nancy Flanagan, NBCT.

MODULE THREE: PROVIDING ETHICAL CANDIDATE SUPPORT

ACTIVITY: REVIEWING ETHICS SCENARIOS (cont'd)

SCENARIO #3

Delores, a candidate in a large urban district, notices that the candidate support coordinator (an NBCT who was hired and is paid by the school district) has subtly selected four candidates (from the group of 30) for special assistance. At their biweekly candidate support meetings, the coordinator takes these candidates into a separate room. One of these four candidates admits to Delores that the coordinator rewrites whole pages of their entries. The district does not yet have one NBCT, even though nearly 60 candidates have attempted the process. The coordinator believes the assessment process benefits all teachers, whether they certify or not, and is desperate to keep the program going.

Is this situation ethical or unethical? Why?

Note: Scenario materials provided and adapted by Nancy Flanagan, NBCT.

MODULE THREE: PROVIDING ETHICAL CANDIDATE SUPPORT

ACTIVITY: REVIEWING ETHICS SCENARIOS (cont'd)

SCENARIO #4

An NBCT in a state with no formal candidate support program develops a mailing offering her services as a support provider. The NBCT has never been part of a candidate support group, and does not have any formal training in candidate support. In fact, this NBCT did not receive any support services during her pursuit of certification. The mailing is sent to 300 districts, through the teachers' association, and the teacher begins an online support program for 12 candidates. The candidates pay $100 each for her help.

Is this situation ethical or unethical? Why?

Note: Scenario materials provided and adapted by Nancy Flanagan, NBCT.

MODULE THREE: PROVIDING ETHICAL CANDIDATE SUPPORT

ACTIVITY: REVIEWING ETHICS SCENARIOS (cont'd)

SCENARIO #5

A university-based candidate support provider is not an NBCT but has attended Candidate Support Provider Training. She is convinced that assessors have the best understanding of "what NBPTS is looking for" and develops a small support program that uses only assessors as mentors. The assessor-mentors she hires (mostly NBCTs) freely share descriptions of videos they've seen and detailed information about how retired prompts were scored. They describe the process of locating evidence to candidates and give specific advice to candidates on constructing what they believe are easy-to-score entries and exercises.

Is this situation ethical or unethical? Why?

Note: Scenario materials provided and adapted by Nancy Flanagan, NBCT.

MODULE THREE: PROVIDING ETHICAL CANDIDATE SUPPORT

ACTIVITY: REVIEWING ETHICS SCENARIOS (cont'd)

SCENARIO #6

Four candidates in a brand new certificate area meet online through a Yahoo group. They break away from the listserv and form their own support group. They read (and "score") all of each other's entries, speculate on how to make good choices, and have lengthy online conversations where they give each other concrete and specific advice. They develop mock assessment center prompts for each other, based on the Certificate Overview, and spend a great deal of time dissecting the actual Assessment Center prompts and their responses after they have completed the testing. Three of the four certify; the fourth misses by five points.

Is this situation ethical or unethical? Why?

Note: Scenario materials provided and adapted by Nancy Flanagan, NBCT.

MODULE THREE: PROVIDING ETHICAL CANDIDATE SUPPORT

ACTIVITY: REVIEWING ETHICS SCENARIOS (cont'd)

SCENARIO #7

A former candidate who didn't certify is bitter about his experience with the assessment process. As a board member in a statewide education organization, he uses this platform to denounce National Board Certification. Some of his comments are clearly opinion ("Going through the process didn't make me a better teacher…I was already a great teacher!"), but some of the things he says publicly are false ("You must be using X — a particular curriculum in order to certify, and our district uses Y, so I wasn't even eligible to pass"). He urges his association to withdraw support for National Board Certification from their formal policy statement and actively campaigns against National Board Certification in his large suburban district.

Is this situation ethical or unethical? Why?

Note: Scenario materials provided and adapted by Nancy Flanagan, NBCT.

Module Three Summary

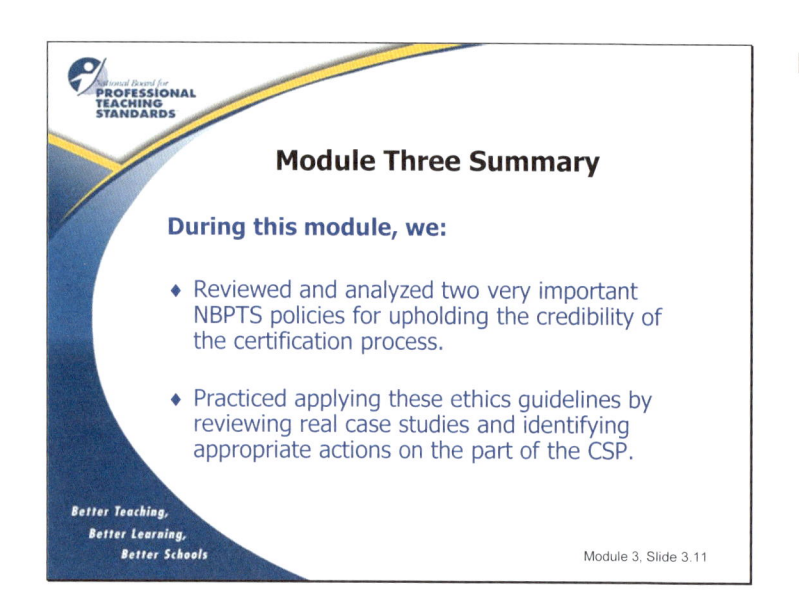

During this module, we:

- Reviewed and analyzed two very important NBPTS policies for upholding the credibility of the certification process.

- Practiced applying these ethics guidelines by reviewing real case studies and identifying appropriate actions on the part of the CSP.

Notes:

# Module Four:
The Scoring Process

Module Four: The Scoring Process

Module Overview

This module provides an overview of the National Board's scoring process for both portfolio entries and assessment center exercises. During this module, you will learn about NBPTS score sites and assessors, scoring safeguards, the score scale, how to read and analyze a score report, and how to prepare candidates for the retake process, if necessary.

Learning Objectives

After completing this module you will be able to:

- Assure candidates that scoring is completed in a controlled environment with carefully trained assessors.

- Articulate the safeguards that the National Board has put in place to protect the process and ensure equity and fairness.

- Explain to candidates the score scale and weights used for scoring portfolio entries and assessment center exercises.

- Help candidates analyze their score report and support them through the retake process, if necessary.

Resources

Some ideas and content in this module were adapted from the following resources:

Accomplished Teaching: The Key to National Board Certification, Bess A. Jennings and MaryAnn D. Joseph, Kendall/Hunt Publishing Company, 2004, pages 203-216

The Teachers Guide to National Board Certification, Adrienne Mack-Kirschner, Heinemann, 2003, page 75.

The National Board Certification Workbook: How to Develop Your Portfolio and Prepare for the Assessment Exams, Adrienne Mack-Kirschner, Heinemann, 2005, page 93.

Navigating the National Board Certification Process, Martha H. Hopkins, Corwin Press, 2004, page 119.

Module Four: The Scoring Process

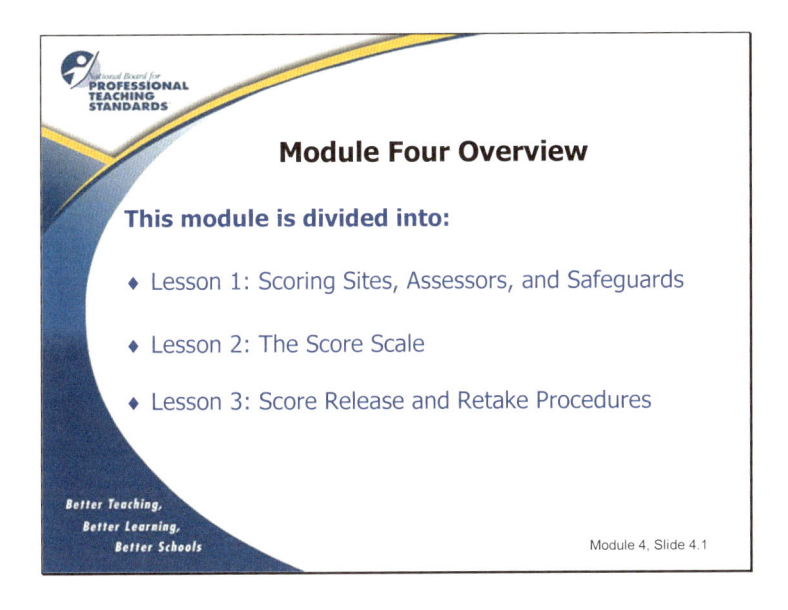

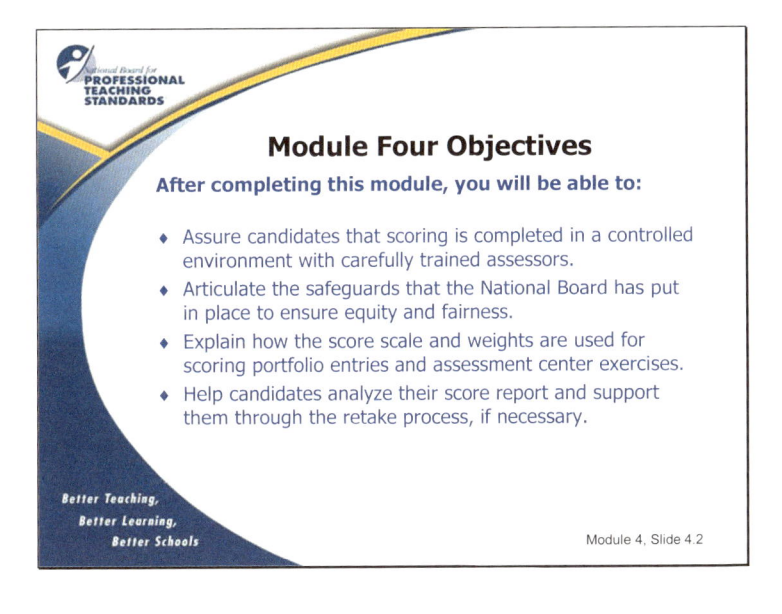

Module Four Overview

This module is divided into:

- Lesson 1: Scoring Sites, Assessors, and Safeguards
- Lesson 2: The Score Scale
- Lesson 3: Score Release and Retake Procedures

Module 4, Slide 4.1

Notes:

Module Four Objectives

After completing this module, you will be able to:

- Assure candidates that scoring is completed in a controlled environment with carefully trained assessors.
- Articulate the safeguards that the National Board has put in place to ensure equity and fairness.
- Explain how the score scale and weights are used for scoring portfolio entries and assessment center exercises.
- Help candidates analyze their score report and support them through the retake process, if necessary.

Module 4, Slide 4.2

Notes:

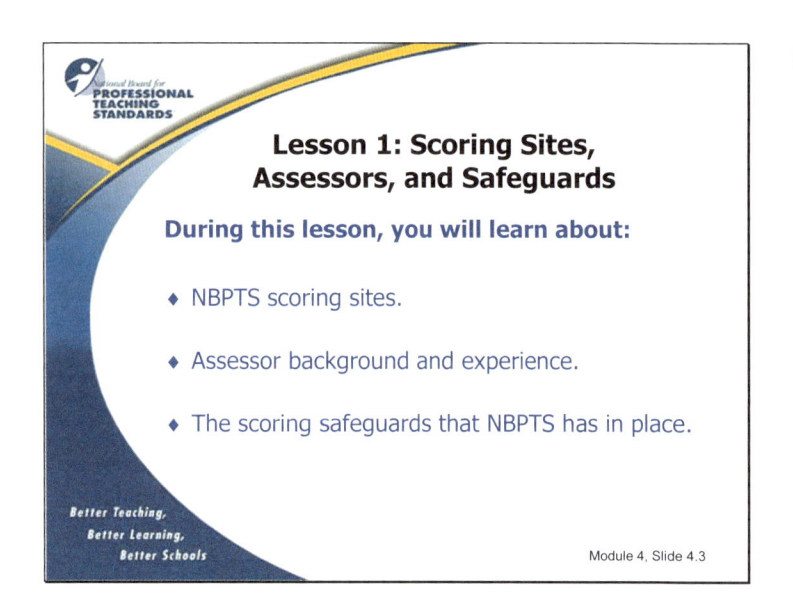

MODULE FOUR: THE SCORING PROCESS

Lesson 1: Scoring Sites, Assessors, and Safeguards

During this lesson, you will learn about:

- NBPTS scoring sites.
- Assessor background and experience.
- The scoring safeguards that NBPTS has in place.

Module 4, Slide 4.3

Notes:

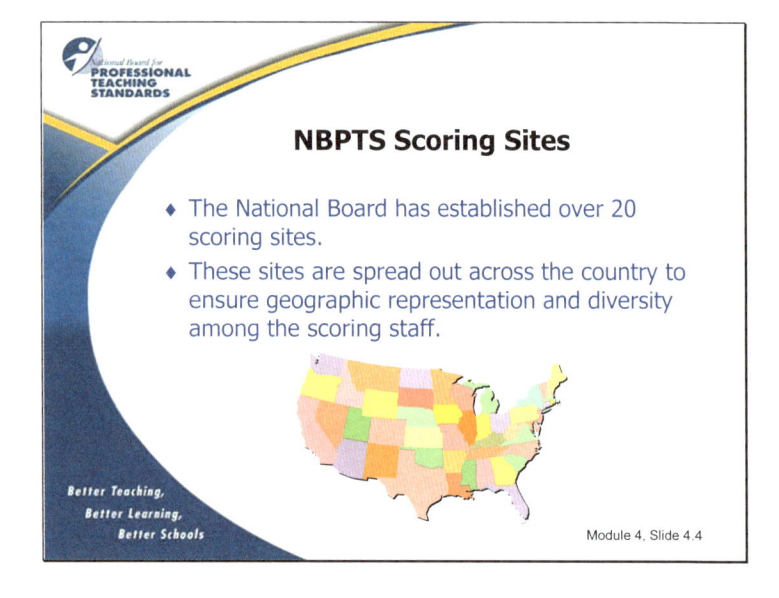

NBPTS Scoring Sites

- The National Board has established over 20 scoring sites.
- These sites are spread out across the country to ensure geographic representation and diversity among the scoring staff.

Module 4, Slide 4.4

Notes:

4.4 NBPTS

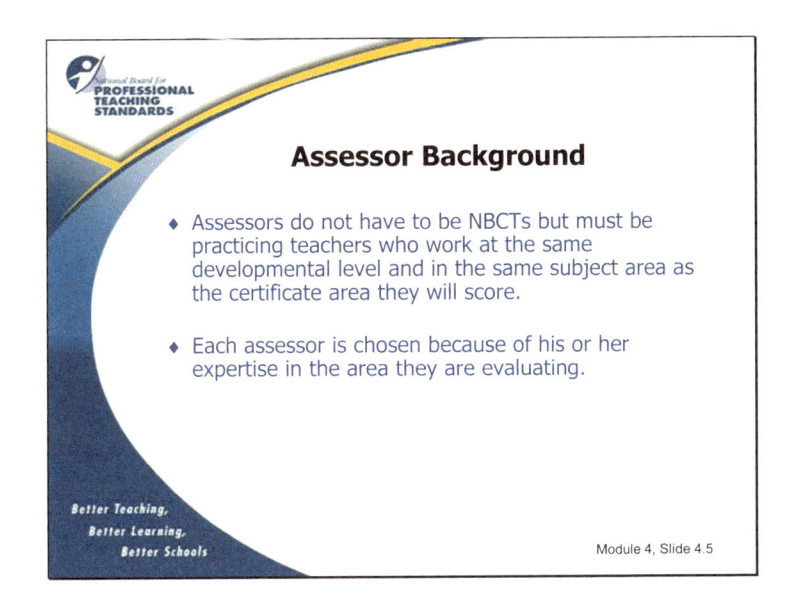

Module Four: The Scoring Process

Assessor Background

- Assessors do not have to be NBCTs but must be practicing teachers who work at the same developmental level and in the same subject area as the certificate area they will score.

- Each assessor is chosen because of his or her expertise in the area they are evaluating.

Module 4, Slide 4.5

Notes:

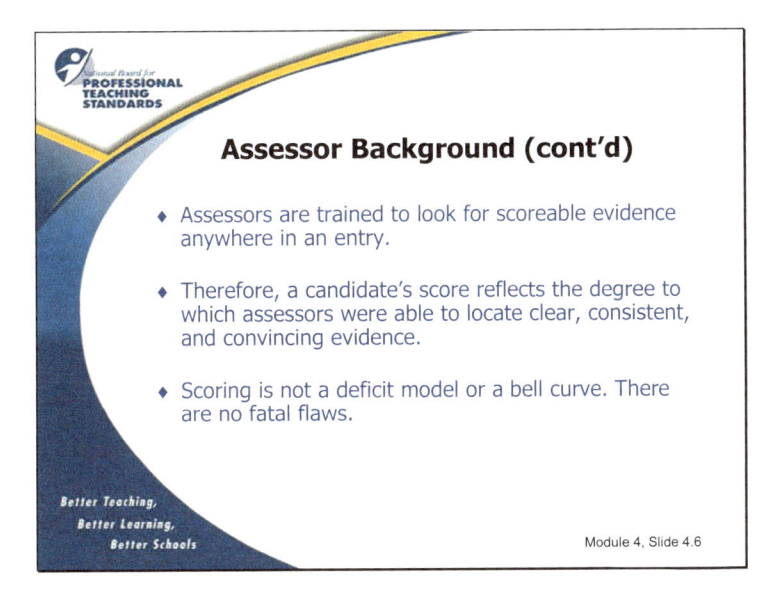

Assessor Background (cont'd)

- Assessors are trained to look for scoreable evidence anywhere in an entry.

- Therefore, a candidate's score reflects the degree to which assessors were able to locate clear, consistent, and convincing evidence.

- Scoring is not a deficit model or a bell curve. There are no fatal flaws.

Module 4, Slide 4.6

Notes:

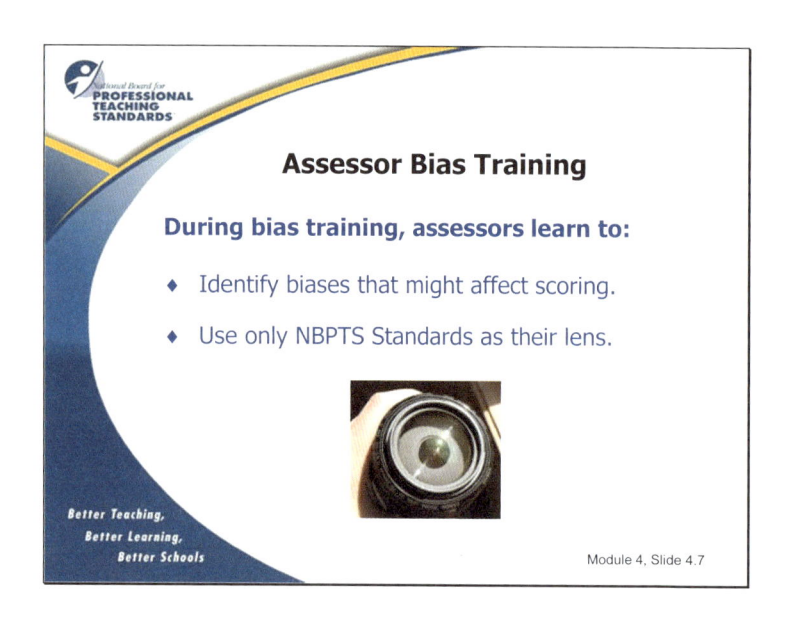

MODULE FOUR: THE SCORING PROCESS

Assessor Bias Training

During bias training, assessors learn to:

- Identify biases that might affect scoring.
- Use only NBPTS Standards as their lens.

Module 4, Slide 4.7

Notes:

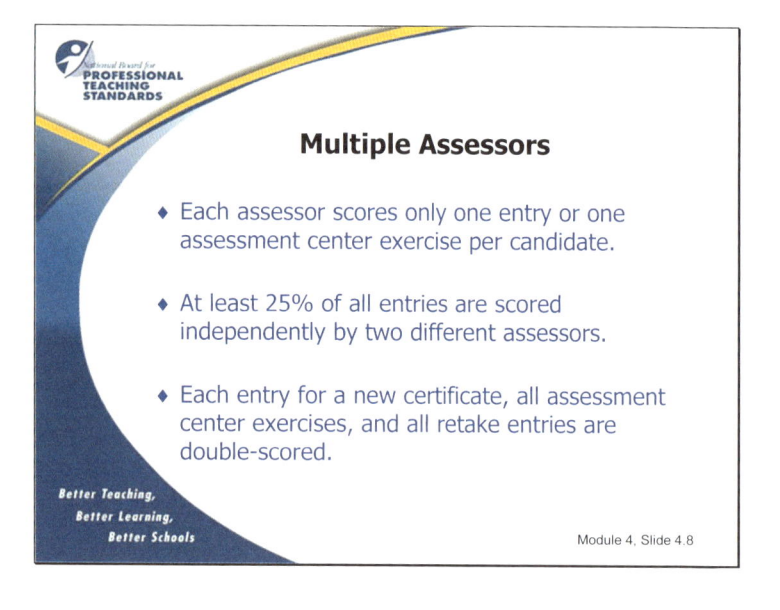

Multiple Assessors

- Each assessor scores only one entry or one assessment center exercise per candidate.
- At least 25% of all entries are scored independently by two different assessors.
- Each entry for a new certificate, all assessment center exercises, and all retake entries are double-scored.

Module 4, Slide 4.8

Notes:

Module Four: The Scoring Process

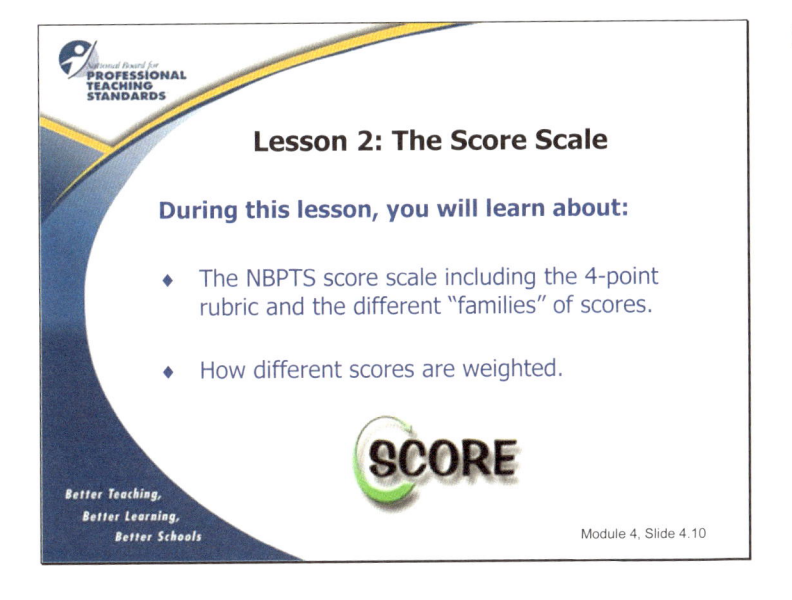

Scoring Safeguards

- All assessors receive the same training.
- The scoring process is reviewed annually by NBPTS to determine the level of assessor reliability.
- These analyses confirm that NBPTS assessors are reliable, accurate, and fair.

Module 4, Slide 4.9

Notes:

Lesson 2: The Score Scale

During this lesson, you will learn about:

- The NBPTS score scale including the 4-point rubric and the different "families" of scores.
- How different scores are weighted.

Module 4, Slide 4.10

Notes:

The 4-Point Rubric

Level 1	Little or No Evidence
Level 2	Limited Evidence
Level 3	Clear Evidence
Level 4	Clear, Convincing, and Consistent Evidence

Notes:

How Certification Is Determined

- Certification is determined by adding the candidate's scores for all 10 sections.
- A 12-point constant is applied for all candidates.
- A minimum total score of **275** is needed to achieve certification.

Notes:

Module Four: The Scoring Process

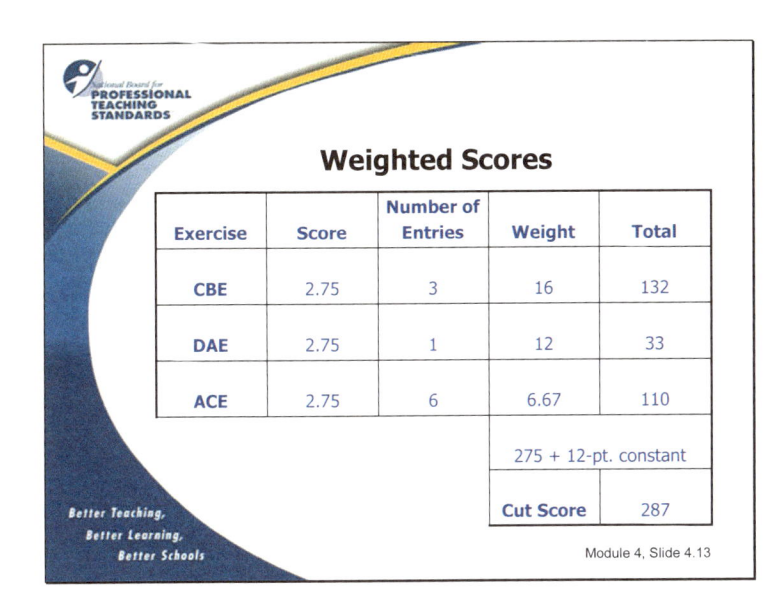

Weighted Scores

Exercise	Score	Number of Entries	Weight	Total
CBE	2.75	3	16	132
DAE	2.75	1	12	33
ACE	2.75	6	6.67	110
			275 + 12-pt. constant	
			Cut Score	287

Module 4, Slide 4.13

Notes:

Lesson 3: Score Release and Retake Procedures

During this lesson, you will learn:

- Where and when scores are released.
- How to read and interpret a score report.
- How to provide support to retake candidates.

Module 4, Slide 4.14

Notes:

MODULE FOUR: THE SCORING PROCESS

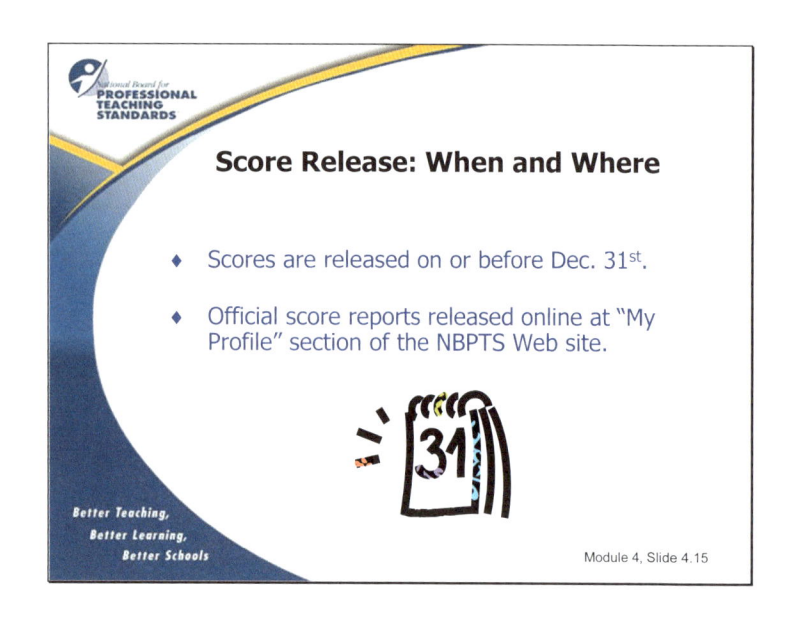

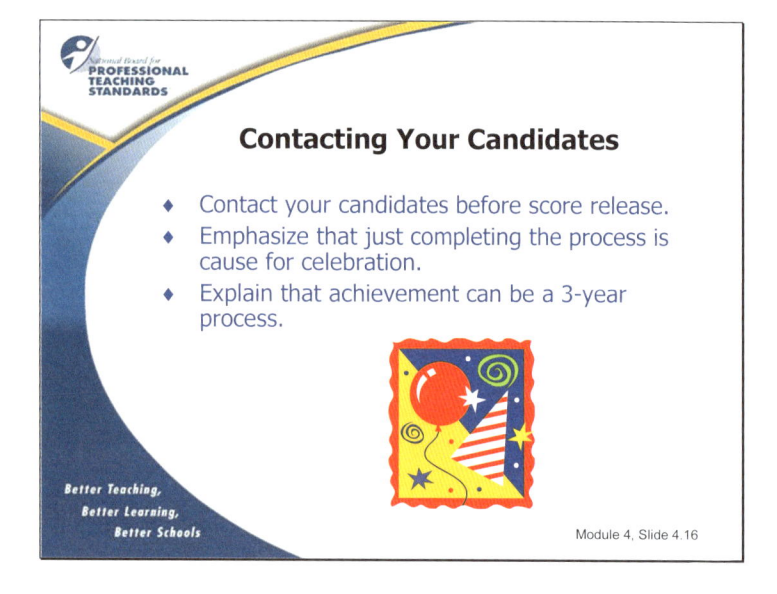

Score Release: When and Where

- Scores are released on or before Dec. 31st.
- Official score reports released online at "My Profile" section of the NBPTS Web site.

Module 4, Slide 4.15

Notes:

Contacting Your Candidates

- Contact your candidates before score release.
- Emphasize that just completing the process is cause for celebration.
- Explain that achievement can be a 3-year process.

Module 4, Slide 4.16

Notes:

Module Four: The Scoring Process

Score Confidentiality

- Don't share the news of candidates' results until the candidates are ready.
- There are reasons why candidates may want to keep their scores to themselves for a period of time.

Better Teaching, Better Learning, Better Schools

Module 4, Slide 4.17

Notes:

Why No Feedback?

- National Board Certification is a professional assessment.
- NBPTS wants candidates to explore on their own where evidence was lacking.
- Scoring is not a deficit model.
- Assessors make no suggestions for improvement.
- The answer to "Why didn't I achieve?" is always the same—not enough evidence was provided.

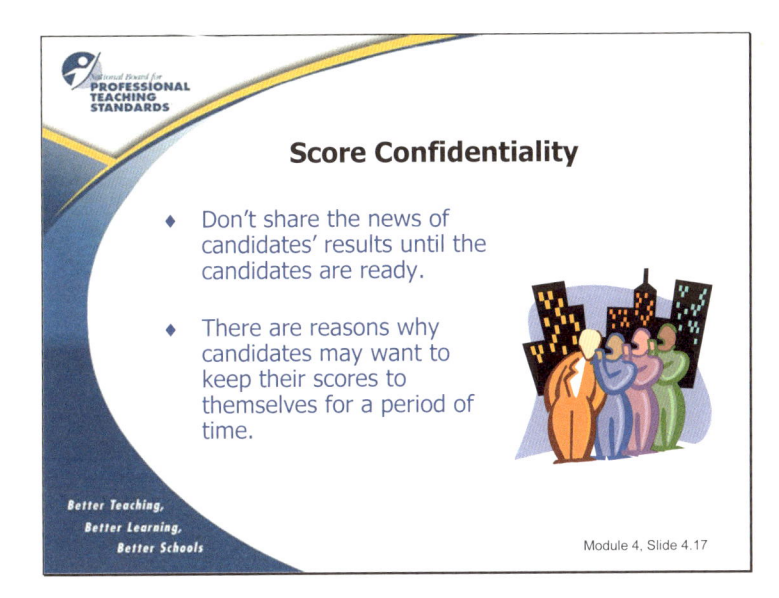

Better Teaching, Better Learning, Better Schools

Module 4, Slide 4.18

Notes:

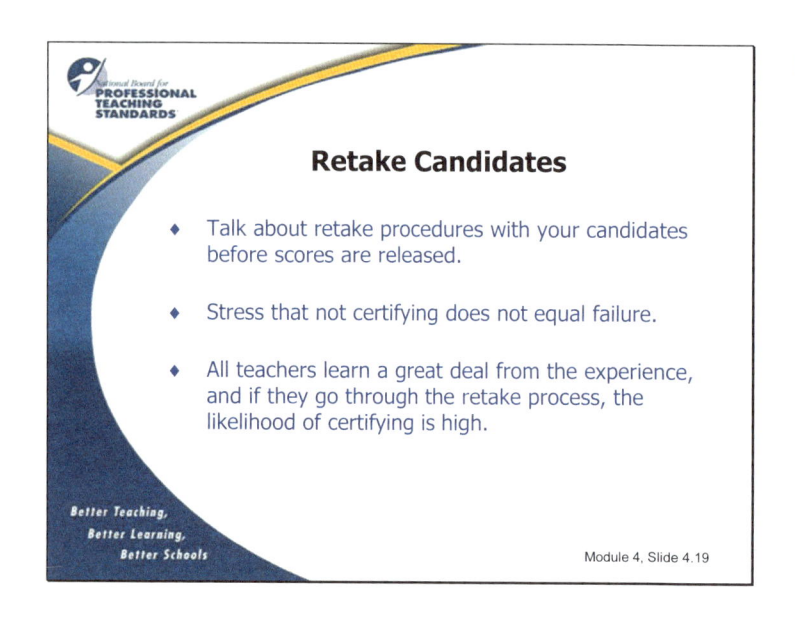

MODULE FOUR: THE SCORING PROCESS

Retake Candidates

- Talk about retake procedures with your candidates before scores are released.
- Stress that not certifying does not equal failure.
- All teachers learn a great deal from the experience, and if they go through the retake process, the likelihood of certifying is high.

Module 4, Slide 4.19

Notes:

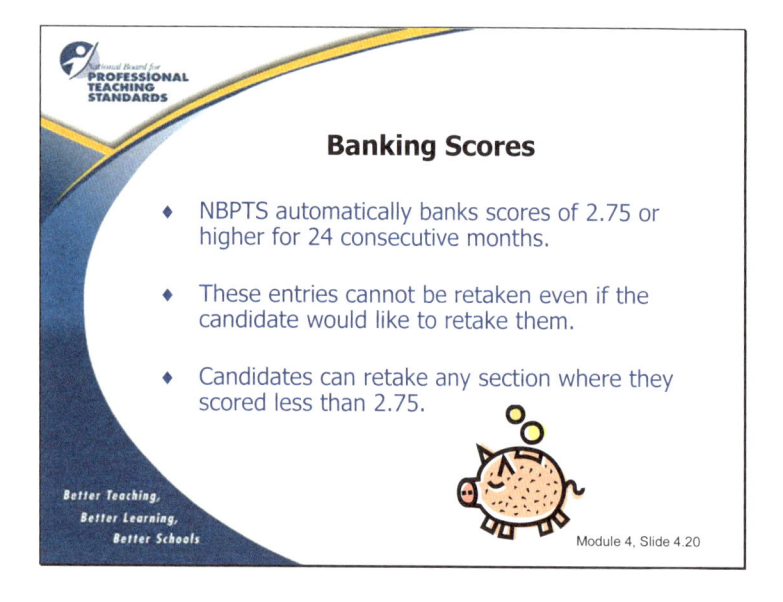

Banking Scores

- NBPTS automatically banks scores of 2.75 or higher for 24 consecutive months.
- These entries cannot be retaken even if the candidate would like to retake them.
- Candidates can retake any section where they scored less than 2.75.

Module 4, Slide 4.20

Notes:

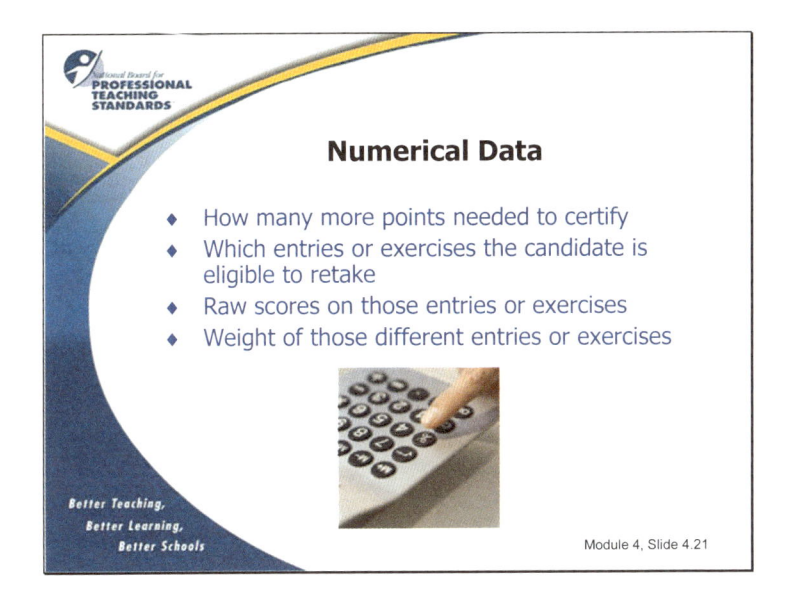

Module Four: The Scoring Process

Numerical Data

- How many more points needed to certify
- Which entries or exercises the candidate is eligible to retake
- Raw scores on those entries or exercises
- Weight of those different entries or exercises

Module 4, Slide 4.21

Notes:

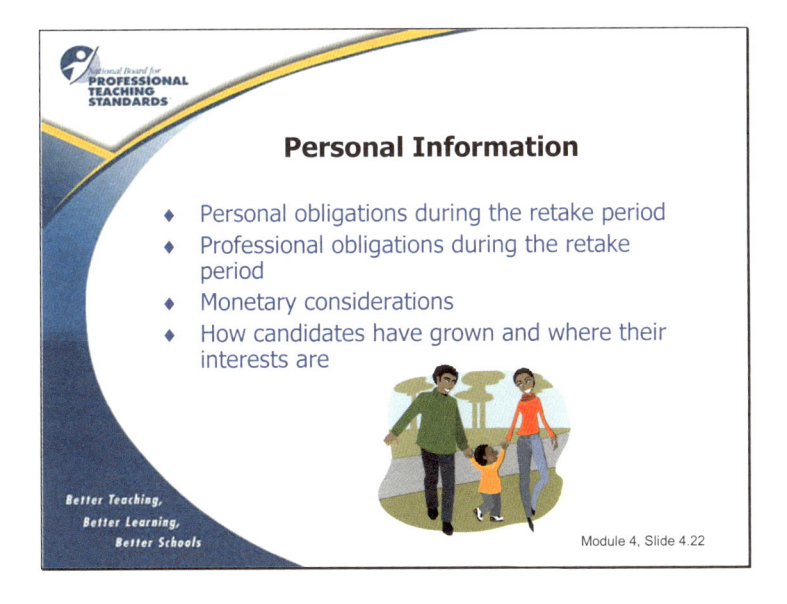

Personal Information

- Personal obligations during the retake period
- Professional obligations during the retake period
- Monetary considerations
- How candidates have grown and where their interests are

Module 4, Slide 4.22

Notes:

MODULE FOUR: THE SCORING PROCESS

Activity

Providing Retake Support

Module 4, Slide 4.23

Notes:

MODULE FOUR: THE SCORING PROCESS

ACTIVITY: PROVIDING RETAKE SUPPORT

PURPOSE:

The purpose of this activity is to provide practice in helping candidates decide which sections they should retake to best improve their chances for certification.

INSTRUCTIONS:

Working with your partner, review the sample score report and the candidate information on the next two pages. Then, answer the questions on **page 4.18.** You may want to refer to the six-step Retake Decision Process on **pages 4.19 and 4.20** and use the worksheet on **page 4.21** of this manual.

Take about **15 minutes** to complete this activity.

MODULE FOUR: THE SCORING PROCESS

ACTIVITY: PROVIDING RETAKE SUPPORT (cont'd)

National Board for PROFESSIONAL TEACHING STANDARDS

Candidate ID:
Certificate: Early and Middle Childhood/Music

To achieve National Board Certification as an Early and Middle Childhood/Music teacher, a candidate must earn a total weighted scaled score on the assessment that equals or exceeds 275.

FULL SCORE PROFILE

Entry or Exercise Name	Raw Exercise Score (RES)	Weight (W)	Weighted Scaled Score (RES X W)
Planning	2.750	16.000	44.00
Delivering Instruction	2.250	16.000	36.00
Demonstrating and Developing Musicianship	2.500	16.000	40.00
Doc Accom: Contrib to Student Learning	2.875	12.000	34.50
Diagnostic Skills	2.750	6.670	18.34
Historical Repertoire	2.675	6.670	17.84
Applied Theory/Composition	2.125	6.670	14.17
Instructional Strategies	2.800	6.670	18.67
Music From a World Sample	2.250	6.670	15.00
Curricular Applications	2.375	6.670	15.84
Sum of Scaled Scores			**255**
Uniform Constant			**12**
TOTAL WEIGHTED SCALED SCORE (TWSS)			**267**

MODULE FOUR: THE SCORING PROCESS

ACTIVITY: PROVIDING RETAKE SUPPORT (cont'd)

Candidate Description:

Personal strengths and weaknesses relative to the certification process: This candidate feels more comfortable responding to portfolio entries where the prompts are known in advance. She performs best when she has ample time to analyze, plan, develop, and edit her written responses. She has carefully reviewed her portfolio entries where she didn't score 2.75 against the scoring rubric and feels confident about what she needs to do to improve her score.

This candidate has a good working knowledge of relevant content in her certificate area which allowed her to perform reasonably well on most of the assessment center exercises. She does however get very anxious about the assessment center exercises because they are timed. She also feels less sure about why she didn't achieve 2.75 on her assessment exercises.

Other influencing factors: This candidate's personal obligations during the retake period are moderate to heavy. She is getting married in six months and was really hoping to certify the first time so she could focus on wedding plans. Also, she is worried about spending more money on the assessment because of the wedding costs. She also has a new principal at her school that is more structured and demanding than the last one and who requires her teachers to show her their lesson plans each week.

ACTIVITY: PROVIDING RETAKE SUPPORT (cont'd)

Questions:

1. How many additional points does this candidate need to certify?

2. Which individual entries and exercises is this candidate eligible to retake?

3. Which of these entries/exercises are weighted most heavily?

4. What are some personal factors this candidate should consider when deciding which pieces to retake?

5. What questions would you ask this candidate regarding retakes?

Module Four: The Scoring Process

ACTIVITY: PROVIDING RETAKE SUPPORT (cont'd)

The Retake Decision Process

On the next few pages is a detailed, six-step process and worksheet that you may want to share with your candidates to help them make sound decisions about what sections of the assessment to retake.

Step 1: Determine how many points your total weighted scaled score differs from the performance standard of 275.

> For example, if you received a TWSS of 268, you need to increase the TWSS by at least 7 points (275 - 268 = 7) to receive National Board Certification.

Step 2: Determine which individual exercises you are eligible to retake.

> Candidates are only eligible to retake exercises on which they scored below a 2.75. These exercises are marked with an asterisk (*) on their score report.

Step 3: Using the worksheet, write down the individual raw exercise scores you received on each of the entries and/or exercises that you are eligible to retake.

> These numbers are located in the raw exercise score column of your score report.

Step 4: Estimate a reasonable score increase that you might attain on each of the individual entries and/or exercises that you are eligible to retake. Write these down.

> What score did you receive on your entries/exercises? The lower the score, the more room for improvement. But if you scored very low on an entry or exercise, you must decide how likely it is that you can improve it significantly. Also, remember the greater the weight associated with a specific entry/exercise, the more impact an increased score will have on your TWSS. Be realistic and consider the factors discussed in Steps 5 and 6.

ACTIVITY: PROVIDING RETAKE SUPPORT (cont'd)

The Retake Decision Process (cont'd)

Step 5: Assess your personal strengths and weaknesses relative to each of the exercises you are eligible to retake.

Consider the following questions:

- Are you more comfortable responding to portfolio entries (where prompts are known in advance) or responding to assessment center exercises (where the prompts are not known in advance)?

- When comparing your portfolio responses to the rubric for the entry, are you clear about why your score is not higher?

- Do you become anxious during timed assessments?

- When comparing your portfolio responses to the rubric for the entry, are you **absolutely clear** about why your score is not higher?

- Do you have good ideas about how to improve your performance on portfolio entries and assessment center exercises?

Step 6: Consider other factors when deciding which individual exercise(s) to retake, including:

- Are you still teaching in the same certificate area?

- What are your personal obligations during the retake timeframe?

- Are your school-related or professional obligations likely to increase, decrease, or remain the same across the retake eligibility period?

- Are your other outside activities likely to increase, decrease, or remain the same?

- Is funding an issue? Remember that each portfolio entry or assessment center exercise you retake will cost $350, so you will want to identify sources of financial assistance if needed.

- How difficult will it be for you to complete the exercise(s) if you delay your retake(s) by a year?

MODULE FOUR: THE SCORING PROCESS

ACTIVITY: PROVIDING RETAKE SUPPORT (cont'd)

Retake Worksheet

Entry/Exercise Name	Weight	Expected New Raw Score	Earned Raw Score	Reasonable Raw Score Increase	Weight x Reasonable Raw Score Increase =
Entry 1	16.00				
Entry 2	16.00				
Entry 3	16.00				
Entry 4	12.00				
ACE 1	6.67				
ACE 2	6.67				
ACE 3	6.67				
ACE 4	6.67				
ACE 5	6.67				
ACE 6	6.67				
Uniform Constant					12
				TOTAL =	

Note: The NBPTS Web site and the candidate CD both contain an electronic exercise for helping candidates make choices about what sections to retake.

Source: The National Board for Professional Teaching Standards Handbook on National Board Certification, Effective 2006

MODULE FOUR: THE SCORING PROCESS

Module Four Summary

During this module, you learned about:

- Scoring sites.
- Assessors.
- The score scale and weights.
- Score release.
- Retakes.

Notes:

Module Five:
Working Effectively with Candidates

Module Five: Working Effectively with Candidates

Module Overview

During this module, you will learn about adult learning principles and how you can apply these principles when working with candidates. You will explore common barriers to effective communication between CSPs and candidates and become skilled in using core interpersonal skills such as attending, questioning, and positive presuppositions.

The latter part of this module presents information on biases and provides guidelines for helping CSPs put their biases aside when supporting candidates.

Learning Objectives

After completing this module you will be able to:

- Apply adult learning principles throughout the CSP process to motivate candidates and help them develop professionally.

- Identify common communication barriers between CSPs and candidates, the consequences of these barriers, and strategies for avoiding them.

- Use effective communication skills to establish rapport and trust, deepen the candidate's level of thinking, and improve their self-confidence.

- Identify your own biases, put them aside, and use the NBPTS Standards to objectively evaluate a candidate's work.

- Explain the importance of valuing and appreciating the individuality of candidates, including unique learning and teaching styles, cultural differences, and level/type of experience.

Resources

Some content and ideas in this module were adapted from the following resources:

The Adult Learner, Malcolm Shepherd Knowles, Ed Holton and Richard A. Swanson, Butterworth-Heinemann, 2005.

Accomplished Teaching: The Key to National Board Certification, Bess A. Jennings and MaryAnn D. Joseph, Kendall/Hunt Publishing Company, 2004, pages 151-159.

The Teachers Guide to National Board Certification, Adrienne Mack-Kirschner, Heinemann, 2003, pages 86-88.

The Art of Helping in the 21st Century, Robert R. Carkhuff, Human Resource Development Press, 1999.

"Change of Heart; Heart of Change Newsletter", December 2006, www.heartofchange.com

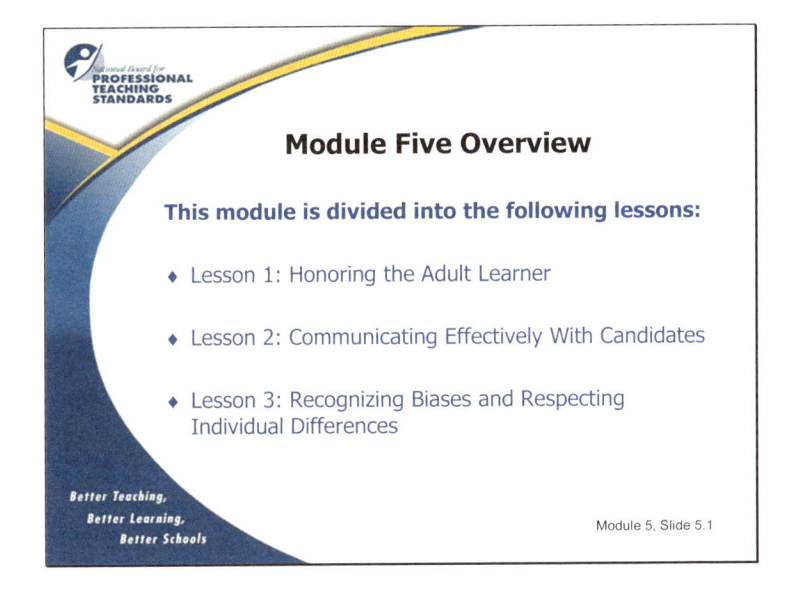

Module Five: Working Effectively with Candidates

Module Five Overview

This module is divided into the following lessons:

- Lesson 1: Honoring the Adult Learner
- Lesson 2: Communicating Effectively With Candidates
- Lesson 3: Recognizing Biases and Respecting Individual Differences

Module 5, Slide 5.1

Notes:

Module Five Objectives

After completing this module, you will be able to:

- Apply adult learning principles throughout the CSP process.
- Identify common communication barriers between CSPs and candidates.
- Use effective communication skills with candidates.
- Recognize and set aside your own biases.
- Explain the importance of valuing and appreciating the individuality of candidates.

Module 5, Slide 5.2

Notes:

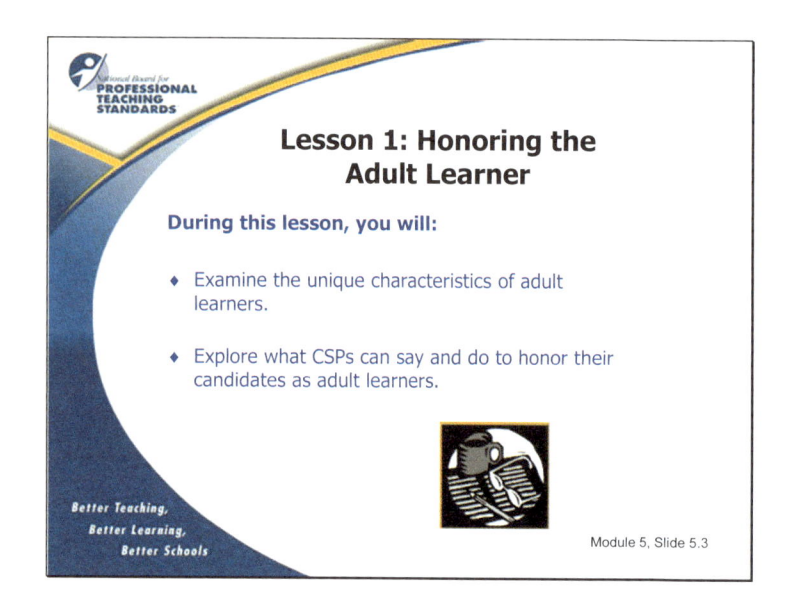

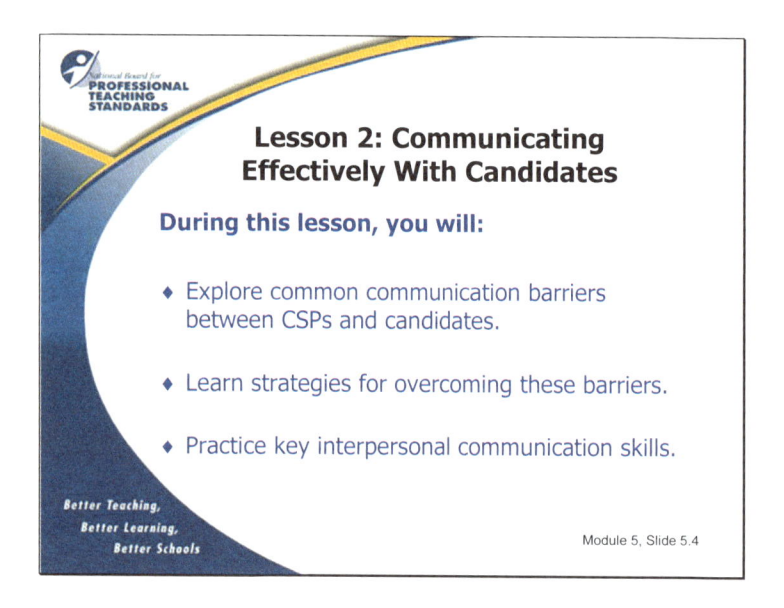

MODULE FIVE: WORKING EFFECTIVELY WITH CANDIDATES

Lesson 1: Honoring the Adult Learner

During this lesson, you will:

- Examine the unique characteristics of adult learners.

- Explore what CSPs can say and do to honor their candidates as adult learners.

Module 5, Slide 5.3

Notes:

Lesson 2: Communicating Effectively With Candidates

During this lesson, you will:

- Explore common communication barriers between CSPs and candidates.

- Learn strategies for overcoming these barriers.

- Practice key interpersonal communication skills.

Module 5, Slide 5.4

Notes:

Module Five: Working Effectively with Candidates

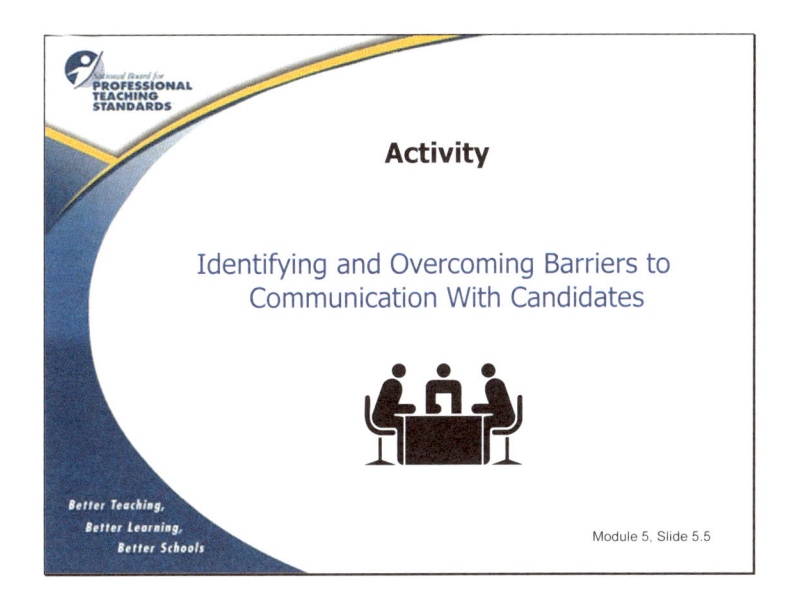

Activity

Identifying and Overcoming Barriers to Communication With Candidates

Module 5, Slide 5.5

Notes:

MODULE FIVE: WORKING EFFECTIVELY WITH CANDIDATES

ACTIVITY: IDENTIFYING AND OVERCOMING COMMUNICATION BARRIERS WITH CANDIDATES

PURPOSE:

The purpose of this activity is to identify barriers to effective communication with candidates, possible consequences of these barriers, and strategies for overcoming them.

INSTRUCTIONS:

Work with your other group members and answer the following three questions:

- What do you think are some common barriers to effective communication between CSPs and candidates?

- What do you think are some negative consequences of these barriers?

- What strategies can CSPs use to overcome these barriers to effective communication with their candidates?

Select a spokesperson to record your responses on your piece of chart paper and share them with the class.

Take about **10 minutes** to complete this activity.

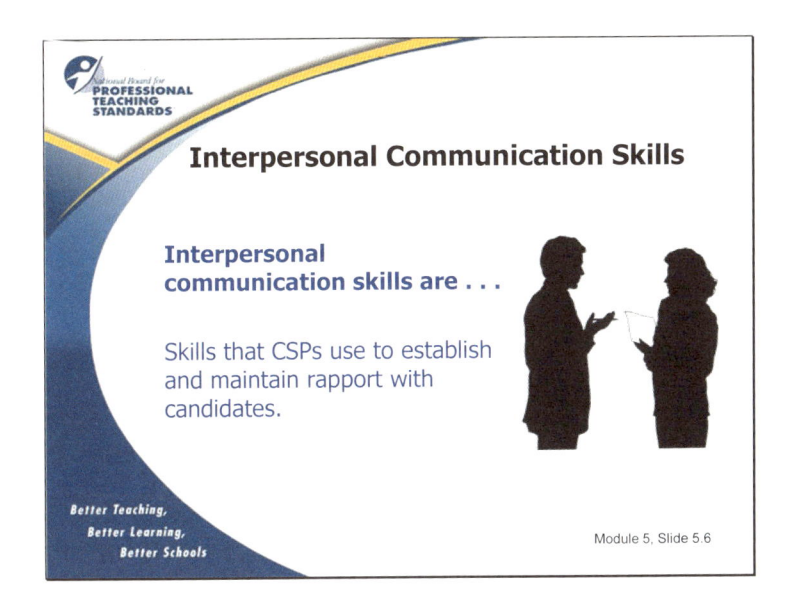

Module Five: Working Effectively with Candidates

Interpersonal Communication Skills

Interpersonal communication skills are . . .

Skills that CSPs use to establish and maintain rapport with candidates.

Module 5, Slide 5.6

Notes:

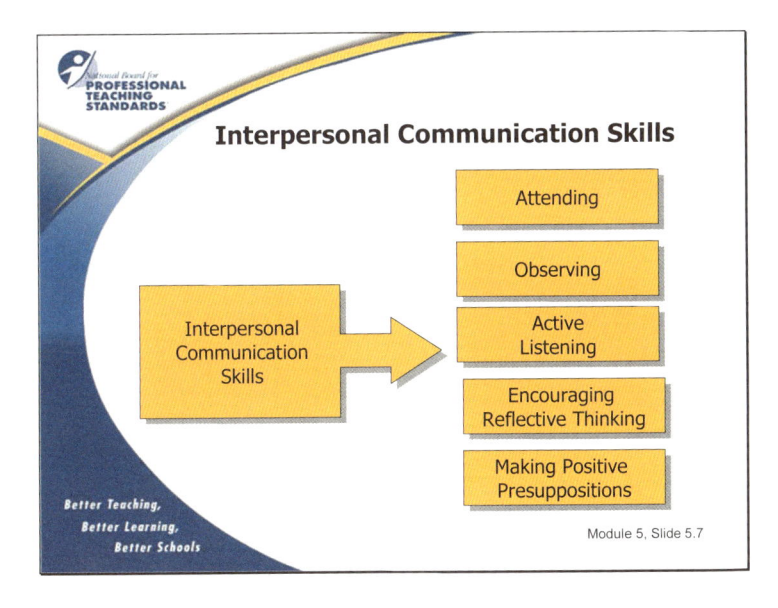

Interpersonal Communication Skills

Interpersonal Communication Skills →
- Attending
- Observing
- Active Listening
- Encouraging Reflective Thinking
- Making Positive Presuppositions

Module 5, Slide 5.7

Notes:

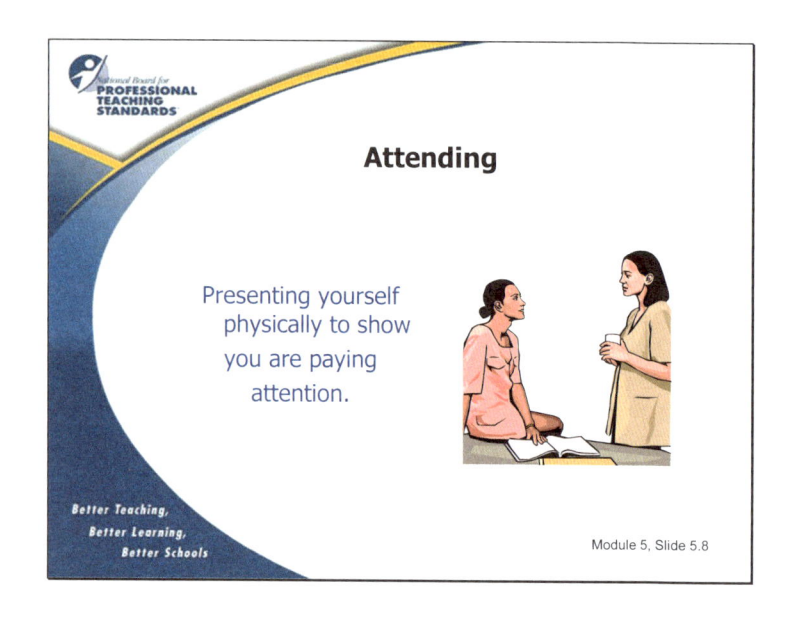

MODULE FIVE: WORKING EFFECTIVELY WITH CANDIDATES

Attending

Presenting yourself physically to show you are paying attention.

Module 5, Slide 5.8

Notes:

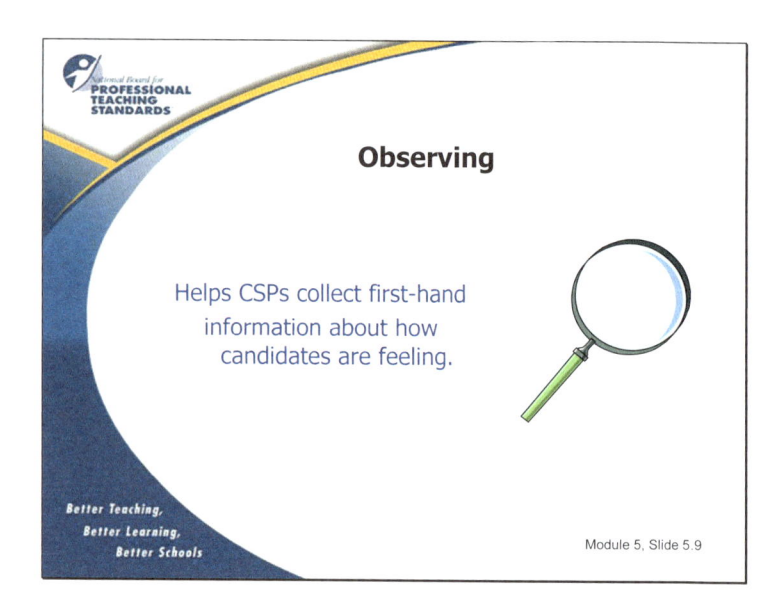

Observing

Helps CSPs collect first-hand information about how candidates are feeling.

Module 5, Slide 5.9

Notes:

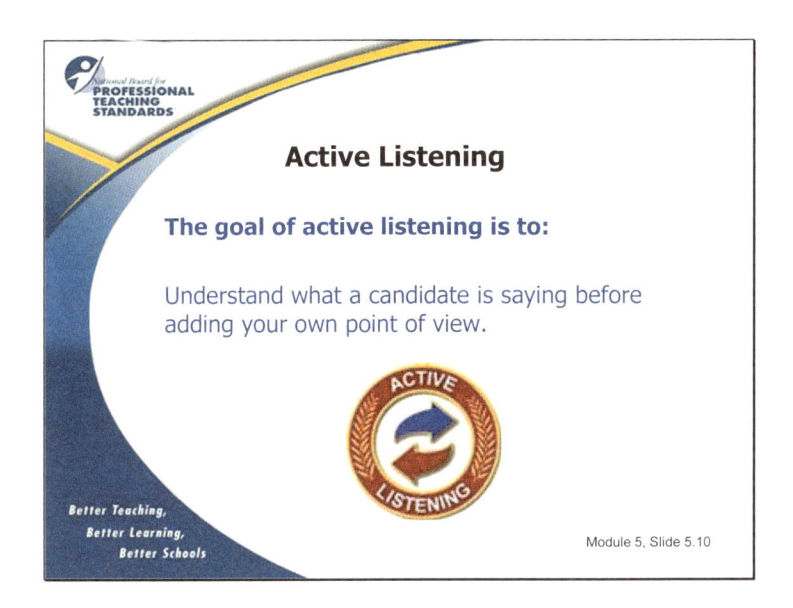

Module Five: Working Effectively with Candidates

Active Listening

The goal of active listening is to:

Understand what a candidate is saying before adding your own point of view.

Module 5, Slide 5.10

Notes:

Two Most Important Communication Skills

- Encouraging reflective thinking through questioning.
- Making positive presuppositions.

Module 5, Slide 5.11

Notes:

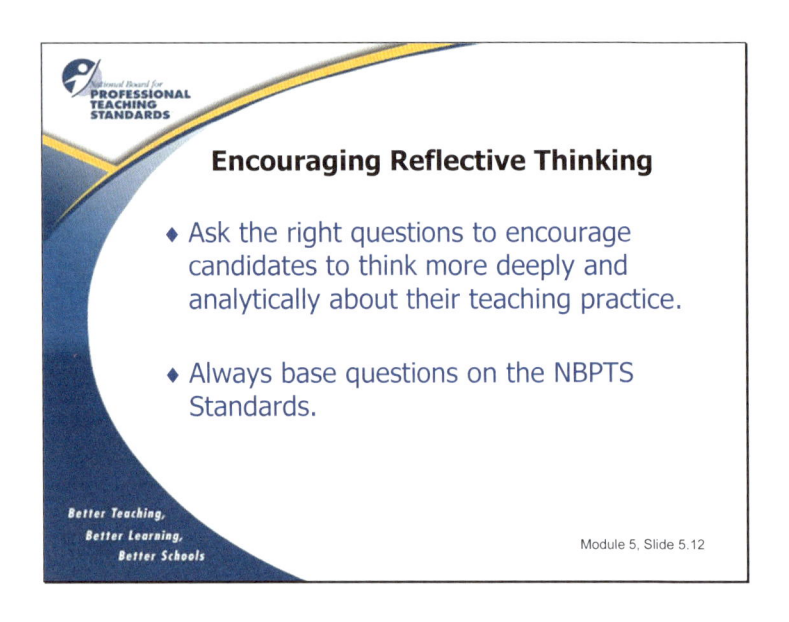

Encouraging Reflective Thinking

- Ask the right questions to encourage candidates to think more deeply and analytically about their teaching practice.

- Always base questions on the NBPTS Standards.

Notes:

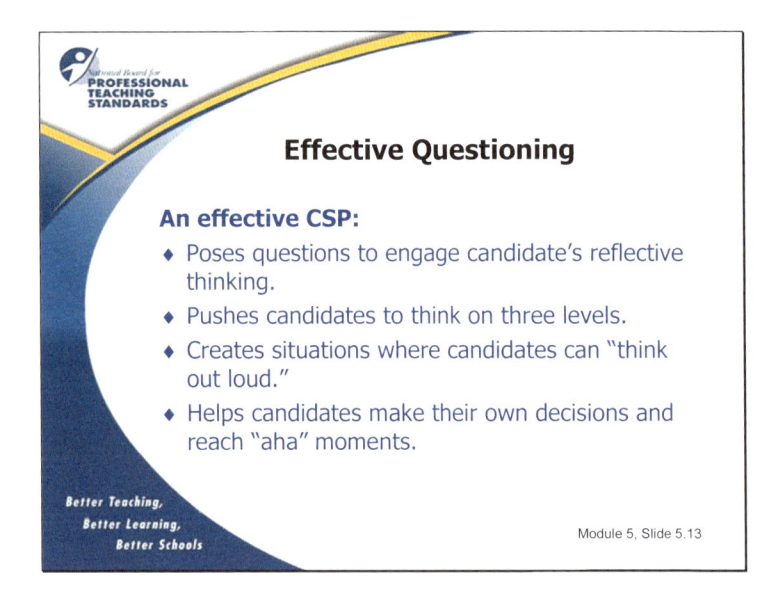

Effective Questioning

An effective CSP:
- Poses questions to engage candidate's reflective thinking.
- Pushes candidates to think on three levels.
- Creates situations where candidates can "think out loud."
- Helps candidates make their own decisions and reach "aha" moments.

Notes:

QUESTIONS THAT PUSH A CANDIDATE'S ANALYTICAL THINKING

Seeking Clarification

- What might be some connection between this and the standards?
- Specifically, what might you mean when you say, "learn ____"?
- How might your students react to the outcome of this lesson?
- How might you know when you've been successful?
- What might you see/hear that will let you know you've reached your goal?

Probing Assumptions

- What assumptions are surfacing for you?
- What might be some other ways to view this?
- As you consider your options, what reasons for your choices become apparent?
- In what ways do your assumptions play out in other areas?
- What are your hunches about why these assumptions are made?

Probing Reasons and Evidence

- What are some examples of evidence supporting that?
- What are some ways you'd back this up with evidence?
- What are some appropriate applications for this case?
- What might be some other ways to support your stance?
- How might you test the evidence you've produced?

Questioning Viewpoints

- What thoughts caused you to choose this over that?
- How might other teachers/parents/people respond to this question?
- What reasons might you give to support your objection to this?
- What might someone who believed ____ think?
- What might be some alternatives you'd like to consider?

QUESTIONS THAT PUSH A CANDIDATE'S ANALYTICAL THINKING (cont'd)

Probing Implications and Consequences

- What implications are you suggesting?
- If this change occurred, what other results might you have?
- What are some effects of this decision?
- If this fits for you, what other things might be true?
- As a candidate who strives for ethical practice, how might this support your beliefs?

Questioning the Question

- What are some assumptions you can make about this question?
- What are your hunches about why you are being asked this question?
- As you think about your response to this question, what thoughts are very clear to you? What are some fuzzy areas you have?
- What other ways might you interpret this question?
- To respond to this question, what other pieces of information do you need?

MODULE FIVE: WORKING EFFECTIVELY WITH CANDIDATES

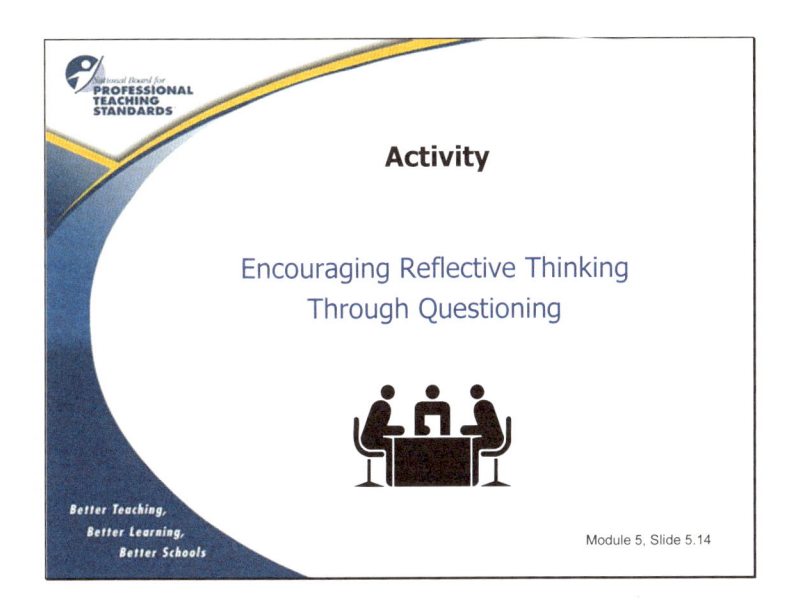

Activity

Encouraging Reflective Thinking Through Questioning

Module 5, Slide 5.14

Notes:

MODULE FIVE: WORKING EFFECTIVELY WITH CANDIDATES

ROLE PLAY ACTIVITY: ENCOURAGING REFLECTIVE THINKING THROUGH QUESTIONING

PURPOSE:

The purpose of this activity is to practice using good questioning techniques to encourage reflective thinking from a candidate.

INSTRUCTIONS:

Read your assigned scenario on the following pages. Each scenario includes an entry question or prompt and then a candidate's response to the question.

With your partner, develop and act out a short conversation between the CSP and candidate. Think about the following when developing your role play:

- What is the candidate's misconception in the scenario?

- What can the CSP say to and ask the candidate to guide a meaningful feedback session and help deepen the candidate's level of thinking about his or her teaching?

Take about **10 minutes** to complete this activity.

MODULE FIVE: WORKING EFFECTIVELY WITH CANDIDATES

ROLE PLAY ACTIVITY: ENCOURAGING REFLECTIVE THINKING THROUGH QUESTIONING (cont'd)

SCENARIO #1

Entry Question:

What about the student as an individual (experiences, skills, and interests) provides insight into his or her work sample and your analysis of him or her?

Candidate Response:

Rodney is a good writer who has had some interesting experiences. His parents lived in Egypt for many years, although Rodney was born after they returned to the U.S. He has a friendly personality but often spends time alone while other students socialize (lunch, breaks). Rodney always likes to write fantasy stories but usually does not write much when he is asked to share his own feelings or opinions.

ROLE PLAY ACTIVITY: ENCOURAGING REFLECTIVE THINKING THROUGH QUESTIONING (cont'd)

SCENARIO #2

Entry Question:

What are the relevant characteristics of this class that influenced your instructional strategies for this lesson: ethnic, cultural, and linguistic diversity; the range of abilities of the students; the personality of the class?

Candidate Response:

This class of 20 eighth graders is 75% female. There are only four white students. Three students are Hispanic, and the rest are African American. One boy is diabetic, and one girl has asthma. All of them speak English. On state end-of-grade tests, all but two of these students scored a three or a four. The students are cooperative and pleasant, but their parents are not involved in their education.

MODULE FIVE: WORKING EFFECTIVELY WITH CANDIDATES

ROLE PLAY ACTIVITY: ENCOURAGING REFLECTIVE THINKING THROUGH QUESTIONING (cont'd)

SCENARIO #3

Entry Question:

To what extent did you achieve the goals you set?

Candidate Response:

All of the goals I set were met completely.

ROLE PLAY ACTIVITY: ENCOURAGING REFLECTIVE THINKING THROUGH QUESTIONING (cont'd)

SCENARIO #4

Entry Question:

Taken in total, what do all of these students' responses say about your strengths and weaknesses as a teacher of reading and writing?

Candidate Response:

The students did a tremendous job at reading and figuring out what the theme of the selection was. This has been very difficult for them in the past, and I'm delighted to see that the light has finally gone on. But while they can figure out the theme, they still cannot carry that skill to their writing. They do not seem to be able to write a story with a theme threaded through it.

MODULE FIVE: WORKING EFFECTIVELY WITH CANDIDATES

ROLE PLAY ACTIVITY: ENCOURAGING REFLECTIVE THINKING THROUGH QUESTIONING (cont'd)

SCENARIO #5

Entry Question:

What are the instructional goals for this particular lesson, and how did you arrive at these goals?

Candidate Response:

The three goals for this lesson are to:

1. Identify sedimentary, igneous, and metamorphic rocks.
2. Make a model of a volcano.
3. Score greater than 85% on a multiple choice test on rocks.

I chose these goals because they fit with the state goals and are important concepts for students this age to learn.

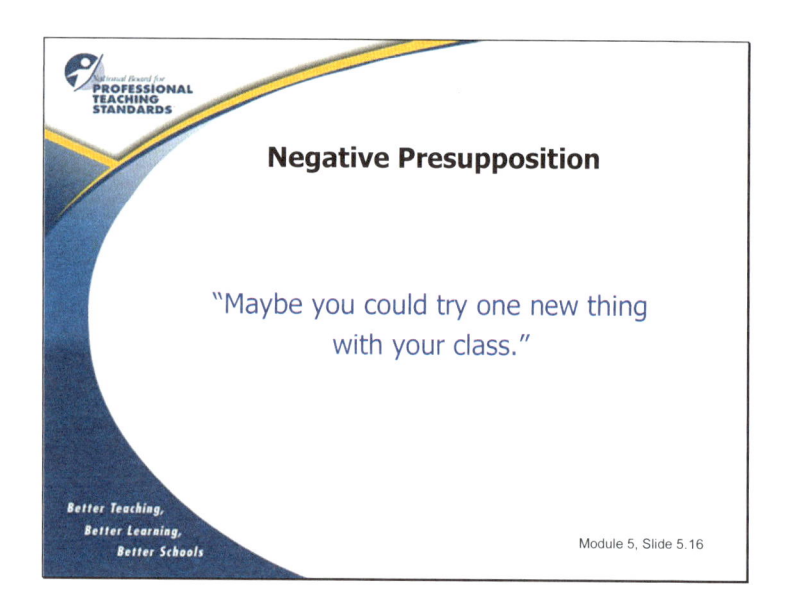

MODULE FIVE: WORKING EFFECTIVELY WITH CANDIDATES

Presuppositions

A presupposition is:

- What a person understands when a statement or question is spoken in addition to what the words actually say.

- Positive or negative.

Module 5, Slide 5.15

Notes:

Negative Presupposition

"Maybe you could try one new thing with your class."

Module 5, Slide 5.16

Notes:

Module Five: Working Effectively with Candidates

Positive Presupposition

"Since you understand the unique needs of your class, which one of the ideas that you are considering will you implement first?"

Module 5, Slide 5.17

Notes:

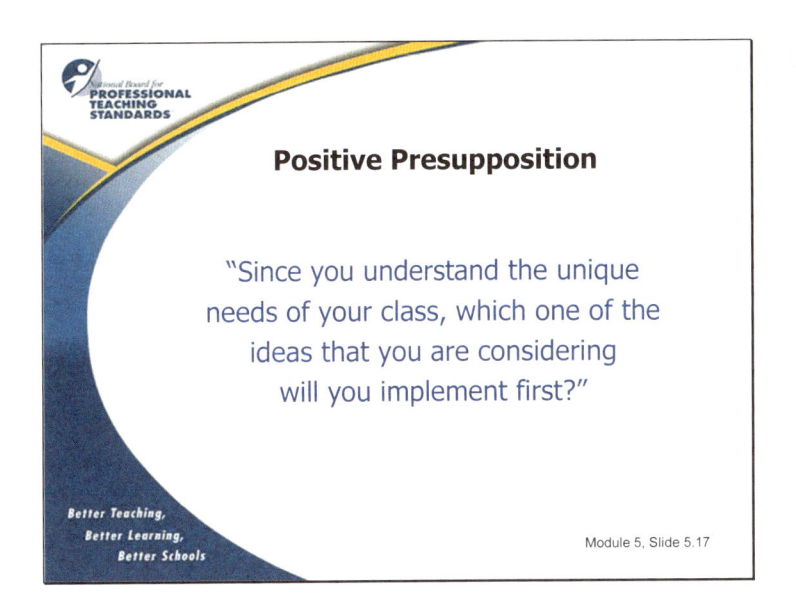

Activity

Role Play Demonstration

Module 5, Slide 5.18

Notes:

ACTIVITY: ROLE PLAY DEMONSTRATION

PURPOSE:

The purpose of this activity is to observe a mock conversation between a CSP and candidate, paying attention to the communication skills used by the CSP and the candidate's responses.

INSTRUCTIONS:

Listen to the mock conversation between the CSP and candidate, paying attention to your assigned area listed below.

- The candidate's misconceptions.
- The CSP's attending and listening skills.
- The CSP's use of good questions.
- The CSP's use of positive presuppositions.
- The candidate's progression of thinking about his/her teaching practice based on the questions.

Jot down notes in the space below about what you hear and observe.

Notes:

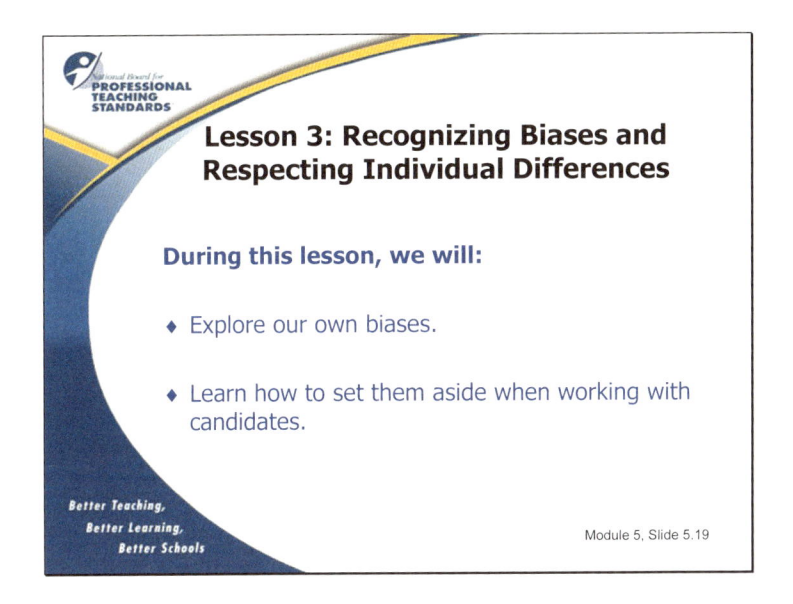

Module Five: Working Effectively with Candidates

Lesson 3: Recognizing Biases and Respecting Individual Differences

During this lesson, we will:

- Explore our own biases.
- Learn how to set them aside when working with candidates.

Module 5, Slide 5.19

Notes:

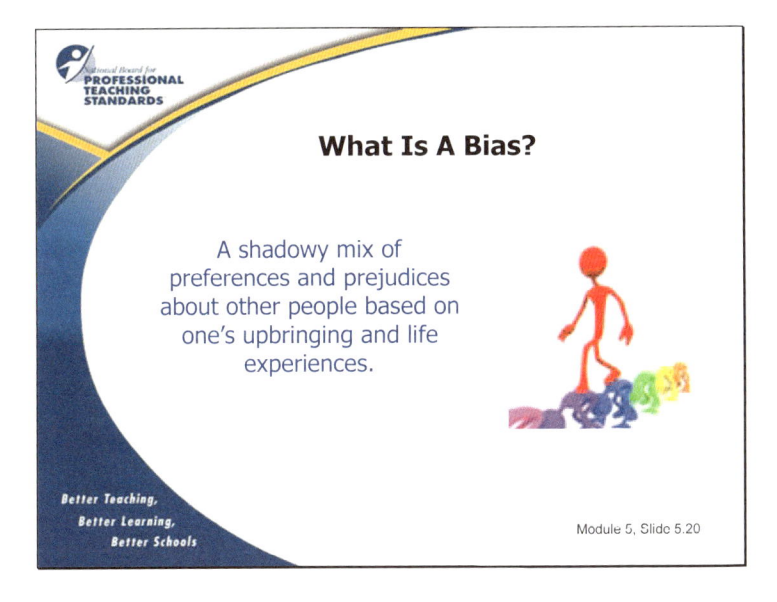

What Is A Bias?

A shadowy mix of preferences and prejudices about other people based on one's upbringing and life experiences.

Module 5, Slide 5.20

Notes:

MODULE FIVE: WORKING EFFECTIVELY WITH CANDIDATES

Activity

Exploring Biases

Module 5, Slide 5.21

Notes:

Module Five: Working Effectively with Candidates

ACTIVITY: EXPLORING BIASES

PURPOSE:

The purpose of this activity is to begin exploring one's biases. **You will not be required to share your responses unless you feel comfortable doing so.**

INSTRUCTIONS:

As the instructor flashes each word on the projection screen, quickly write down the first three thoughts that come to mind below. When you are finished, look back at your responses and think about any potential sources of bias such as personal experience, family experience, community, society, etc.

Thought 1	Thought 2	Thought 3

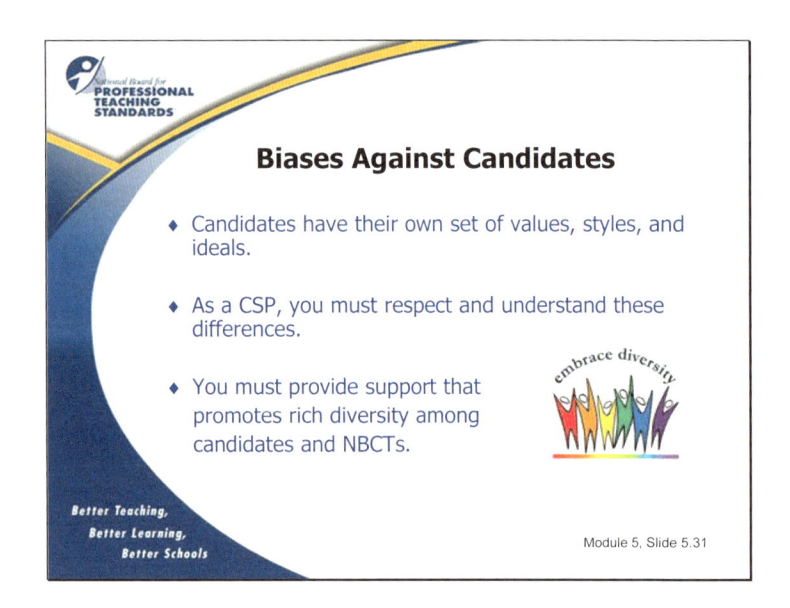

MODULE FIVE: WORKING EFFECTIVELY WITH CANDIDATES

Biases Against Candidates

- Candidates have their own set of values, styles, and ideals.
- As a CSP, you must respect and understand these differences.
- You must provide support that promotes rich diversity among candidates and NBCTs.

Module 5, Slide 5.31

Notes:

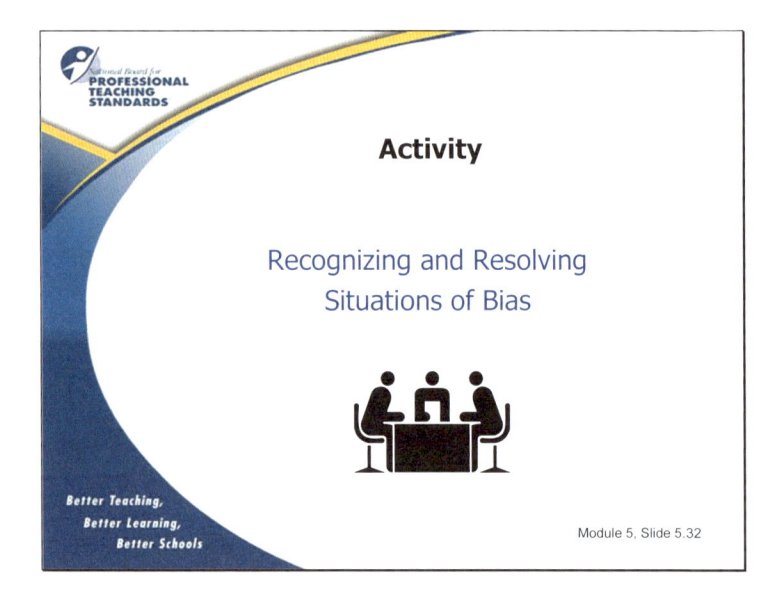

Activity

Recognizing and Resolving Situations of Bias

Module 5, Slide 5.32

Notes:

Module Five: Working Effectively with Candidates

ACTIVITY: RECOGNIZING AND RESOLVING SITUATIONS OF BIAS

PURPOSE:

The purpose of this activity is to examine and discuss real-life candidate support situations that deal with issues of bias and diversity.

INSTRUCTIONS:

Working with your group members, review your assigned scenario (contained on the following pages) and identify the different biases that could surface for the CSP in this situation.

Select a volunteer to record your responses on chart paper and present your results to the class.

Take about **5 minutes** to complete this activity.

MODULE FIVE: WORKING EFFECTIVELY WITH CANDIDATES

ACTIVITY: RECOGNIZING AND RESOLVING SITUATIONS OF BIAS (cont'd)

SCENARIO #1

A middle-aged man wearing sandals, a T-shirt, and jeans sits on a desk, with a racially mixed class of high school students circled in chairs around him. He is bearded, has shoulder-length hair, and wears a bandana. A close-up reveals a snake tattoo on his forearm. He is leading a lively discussion on "Othello" and, while it is clear he knows the play and Shakespeare very well, his discussion questions are somewhat provocative in terms of the racial tension and sexual insinuations in the text.

What biases could surface for a candidate support provider in this situation?

Note: Scenario materials provided and adapted by Nancy Flanagan, NBCT.

Module Five: Working Effectively with Candidates

ACTIVITY: RECOGNIZING AND RESOLVING SITUATIONS OF BIAS (cont'd)

> ### SCENARIO #2
>
> A teacher writes three pages about her under-resourced and impoverished school and students, including detailed statistics on free and reduced-cost lunch count, single parents, neighborhood crime, etc. She details a number of discipline problems with rebellious and disobedient students and difficulties with parent apathy. She writes with some compassion and empathy for the students and stresses her belief that "structured" learning experiences are optimal for children in these environments. The video shows a large, bright, and modern classroom, with a TV monitor, overhead projector, piano, and library corner. Students are seated at tables. The teacher teaches a do-what-I-say lesson using a worksheet, giving students very slow, detailed, and concrete directions ("Look at number one. Point to number one. Copy the number in the blank box," etc.). No student speaks out of turn. In fact, the students are silent. The teacher is white. All of the students are African American.

What biases could surface for a candidate support provider in this situation?

Note: Scenario materials provided and adapted by Nancy Flanagan, NBCT.

ACTIVITY: RECOGNIZING AND RESOLVING SITUATIONS OF BIAS (cont'd)

> **SCENARIO #3**
>
> The video displays a very colorful science classroom, with what appear to be papier-mâché animals suspended from the ceiling, along with paper clouds. Large motivational posters cover the walls, featuring more animals and "cute" slogans. The walls are lined with cages and aquariums, and there is a jar of Tootsie Roll Pops on the podium. The teacher, Mrs. Williams— a jovial, good-natured woman with bright red glasses—moves around the classroom, chatting with her talkative students, who are grouped in fours at microscope stations. The class is AP Biology, in a large suburban high school known for its high statewide test and SAT scores.

What biases could surface for a candidate support provider in this situation?

Note: Scenario materials provided and adapted by Nancy Flanagan, NBCT.

MODULE FIVE: WORKING EFFECTIVELY WITH CANDIDATES

ACTIVITY: RECOGNIZING AND RESOLVING SITUATIONS OF BIAS (cont'd)

SCENARIO #4

The middle-aged male teacher, with a crew-cut and a short-sleeved shirt and tie, is teaching a class of middle school students a lesson on an important battle in the Civil War, using diagrams, arrows and charts on an overhead projector, with accompanying worksheets. A pony-tailed girl who has been "drifting" asks a question about the Civil War that clearly is not relevant to the teacher's lecture. The teacher replies: "Was I talking about that just now? If you weren't paying attention, I'm not going to bore the rest of the class by going back."

What biases could surface for a candidate support provider in this situation?

Note: Scenario materials provided and adapted by Nancy Flanagan, NBCT.

ACTIVITY: RECOGNIZING AND RESOLVING SITUATIONS OF BIAS (cont'd)

SCENARIO #5

A young woman who is in her 4th year of teaching teaches a high school British literature class in a very small, private school in a Northeastern state, where students wear blazers and ties. There are six students in her class. The student work samples submitted by the teacher are outstanding. The teacher clearly has a well-articulated plan for teaching narrative and expository writing, and provides clear evidence of improvement in all the students she features.

What biases could surface for a candidate support provider in this situation?

Note: Scenario materials provided and adapted by Nancy Flanagan, NBCT.

MODULE FIVE: WORKING EFFECTIVELY WITH CANDIDATES

ACTIVITY: RECOGNIZING AND RESOLVING SITUATIONS OF BIAS (cont'd)

SCENARIO #6

Mrs. Jones teaches a large class of third graders in what appears to be an old and crumbling building. Chunks of plaster are missing, and buckets collect dripping water. Her students are seated in a double U-shaped arrangement. As the camera pans back, we see single desks in the far corners of the room, nearly concealed by low bookcases. There are students (both boys) seated at these desks as her math lesson proceeds. One of these boys throws a pencil at the back of another student's head. The teacher instructs the boy to come forward and write his name on the blackboard. He adds his name to a list. Some of the names have several checkmarks and the teacher comments on the number of students whose parents will be called at the end of the day. In the written commentary, the teacher writes enthusiastically about the packaged discipline program she has used with great success for a number of years.

What biases could surface for a candidate support provider in this situation?

Note: Scenario materials provided and adapted by Nancy Flanagan, NBCT.

ACTIVITY: RECOGNIZING AND RESOLVING SITUATIONS OF BIAS (cont'd)

SCENARIO #7

A high school teacher is conducting a lesson on civics with juniors in a school located in an urban area where 100% of the students qualify for free or reduced-cost lunch. He is using a sports quiz show format, with teams of students answering questions on American government. The questions are about bits of information, dates, and terms. The game generates a lot of enthusiasm and shouting of answers; the teacher uses a basketball scoreboard and passes a ball to students to begin new rounds of questioning. In his portfolio entry, the teacher submits the list of facts and terms the students must memorize to play the game successfully. The class is "Advanced Placement Government."

What biases could surface for a candidate support provider in this situation?

Note: Scenario materials provided and adapted by Nancy Flanagan, NBCT.

MODULE FIVE: WORKING EFFECTIVELY WITH CANDIDATES

ACTIVITY: RECOGNIZING AND RESOLVING SITUATIONS OF BIAS (cont'd)

SCENARIO #8

A first grade teacher is shown teaching a lesson on simple machines, using packets of information. The packets show the machines in large, colored illustrations, with arrows and lines indicating energy flow and motion. The students copy simple answers in the packets as the teacher tells them what to write. In her commentary, the teacher notes that the district adopted a uniform elementary science curriculum to boost statewide assessment test scores, and she is required to use these materials.

What biases could surface for a candidate support provider in this situation?

Note: Scenario materials provided and adapted by Nancy Flanagan, NBCT.

Module Five Summary

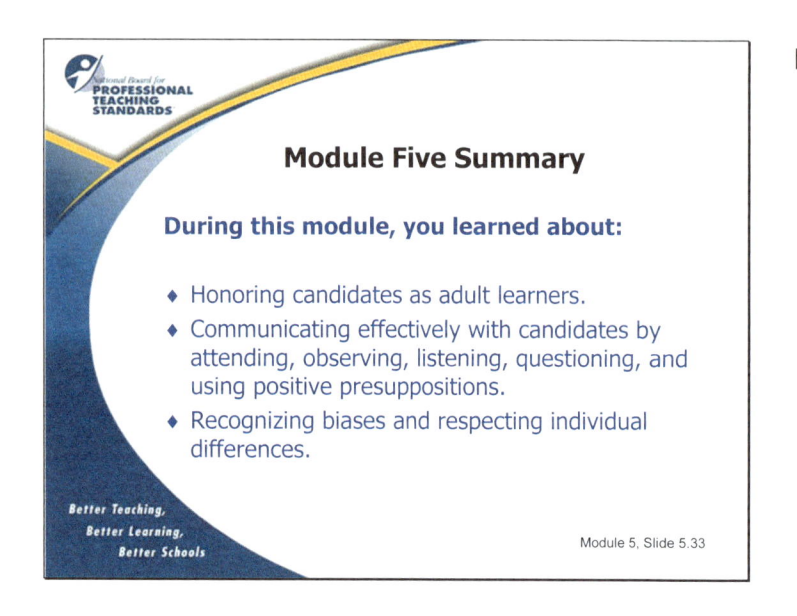

During this module, you learned about:

- Honoring candidates as adult learners.
- Communicating effectively with candidates by attending, observing, listening, questioning, and using positive presuppositions.
- Recognizing biases and respecting individual differences.

Module 5, Slide 5.33

Notes:

Module Six:
Portfolio Entry Review

Module Six: Portfolio Entry Review

Module Overview

The overall goal of this module is to provide you with the knowledge and skills needed to help your candidates during the portfolio development process. During this module, you will learn about the overall role of entry reviewers and gain an understanding about the difficulty and weight of this task.

You will be introduced to the three levels of thinking required in the portfolio entry process and will practice identifying each type of thinking. Next, you will learn how to thoroughly prepare yourselves for the entry review process, including collecting the right background materials and analyzing these materials ahead of time. In Lesson 4, you will be guided through how to read and take notes on an entry, develop the right questions for candidates, and conduct a productive and professional feedback session with candidates.

At the end of this module, you will review an entire portfolio entry, taking notes on evidence, identifying connections between different parts of the entry, and developing questions to ask the candidate.

Learning Objectives

After completing this module you will be able to:

- Describe the overall roles and responsibilities of portfolio entry reviewers and decide if this role is appropriate for you.

- Identify the three levels of thinking that entries require and help candidates move beyond the descriptive level to analytical and reflective thinking.

- Adequately prepare yourself for entry review by collecting, analyzing, and understanding all supporting materials.

- Identify standards-based evidence, logical connections between evidence, and what is lacking in an entry.

- Develop questions and have a professional conversation with candidates to help them reflect on their teaching practice and determine for themselves how to provide more evidence.

Resources

Some ideas and content in this module were adapted from the following resources:

Accomplished Teaching: The Key to National Board Certification, Bess A. Jennings and MaryAnn D. Joseph, Kendall/Hunt Publishing Company, 2004, pages 83-84

Navigating the National Board Certification Process, Martha H. Hopkins, Corwin Press, 2004, pages 29-38.

Module Six: Portfolio Entry Review

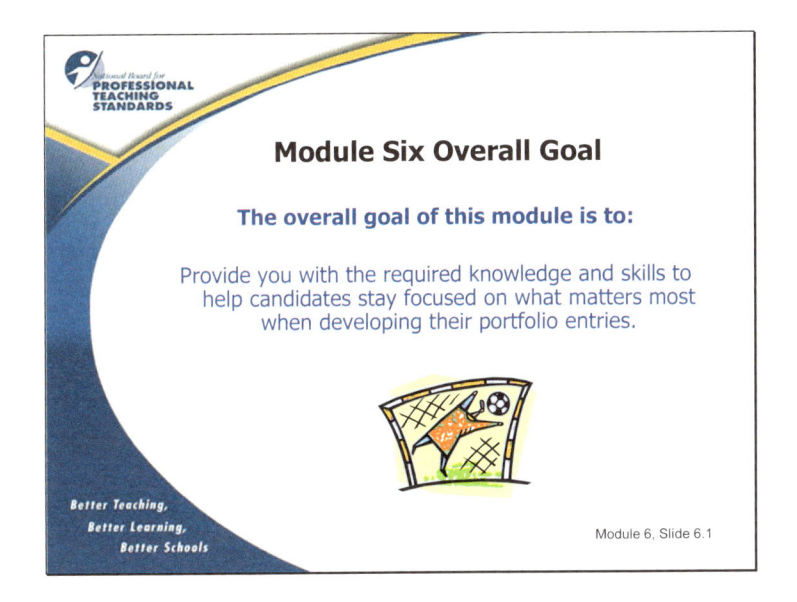

Module Six Overall Goal

The overall goal of this module is to:

Provide you with the required knowledge and skills to help candidates stay focused on what matters most when developing their portfolio entries.

Notes:

Module Six Overview

This module is divided into the following lessons:

- Lesson 1: An Introduction to Entry Review
- Lesson 2: The Thinking Process
- Lesson 3: Preparing for Entry Review
- Lesson 4: Reviewing an Entry
- Lesson 5: Practice and Application

Notes:

MODULE SIX: PORTFOLIO ENTRY REVIEW

Module Six Objectives

After completing this module, you will be able to:

- Describe the overall roles and responsibilities of entry reviewers.
- Identify the three levels of thinking that entries require.
- Prepare yourself for the task of reviewing entries.
- Identify evidence, connections between evidence, and what is lacking in an entry.
- Develop questions and have a professional conversation with candidates to help elevate their level of thinking.

Module 6, Slide 6.3

Notes:

Lesson 1: An Introduction to Portfolio Entry Review

During this lesson, you will:

- Discuss the benefits of portfolio entry review.
- Explore common fears around the role of the entry reviewer and how to alleviate these fears.

Module 6, Slide 6.4

Notes:

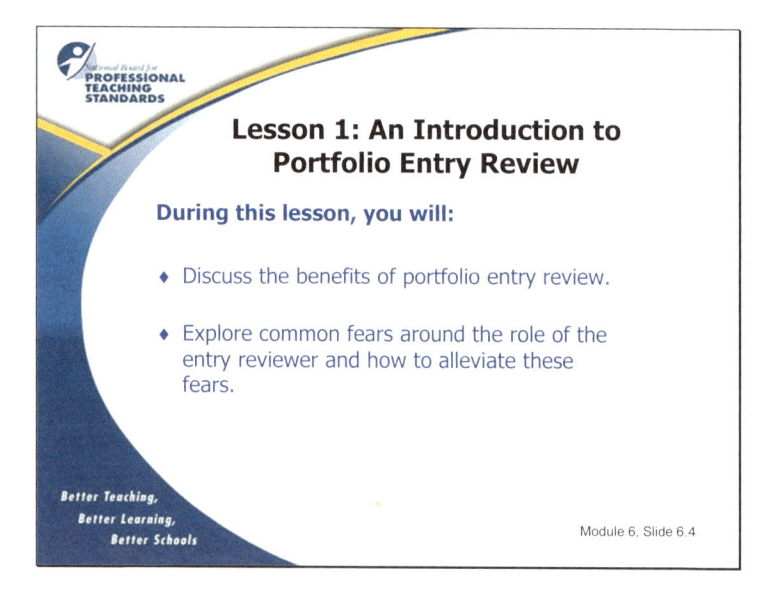

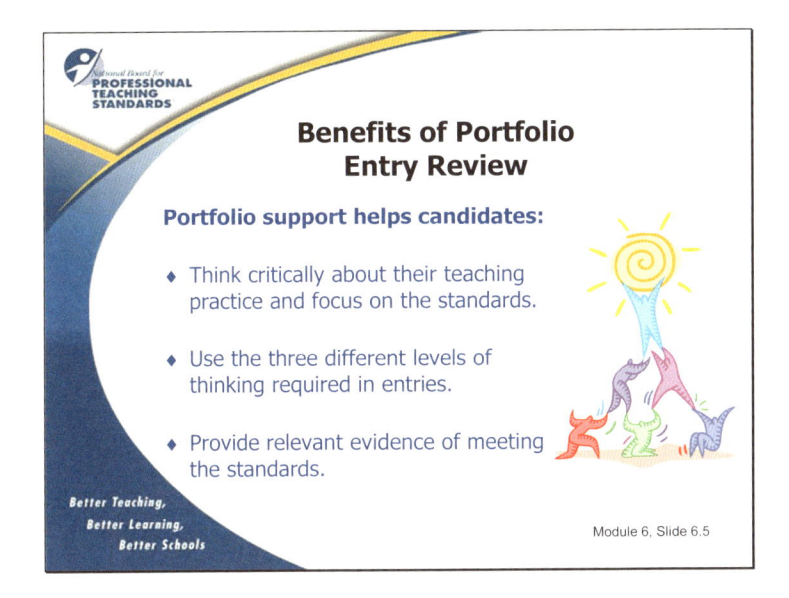

Module Six: Portfolio Entry Review

Benefits of Portfolio Entry Review

Portfolio support helps candidates:

- Think critically about their teaching practice and focus on the standards.
- Use the three different levels of thinking required in entries.
- Provide relevant evidence of meeting the standards.

Module 6, Slide 6.5

Notes:

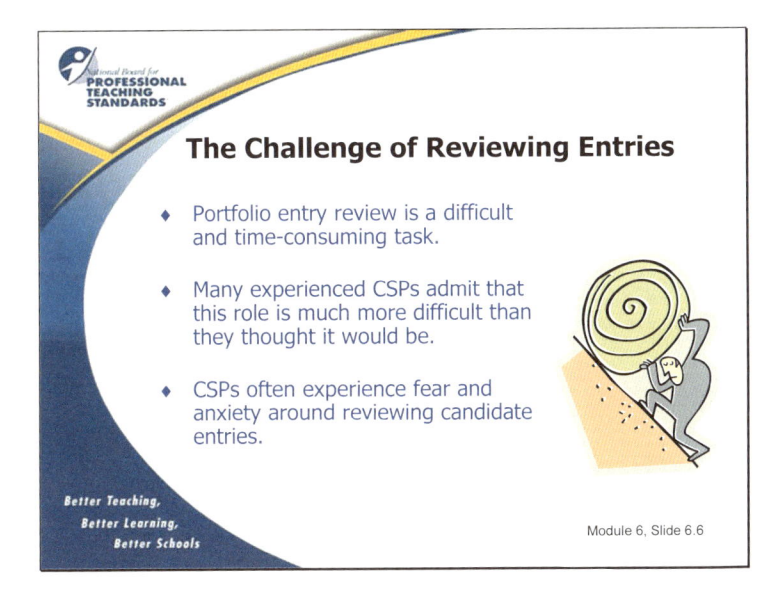

The Challenge of Reviewing Entries

- Portfolio entry review is a difficult and time-consuming task.
- Many experienced CSPs admit that this role is much more difficult than they thought it would be.
- CSPs often experience fear and anxiety around reviewing candidate entries.

Module 6, Slide 6.6

Notes:

MODULE SIX: PORTFOLIO ENTRY REVIEW

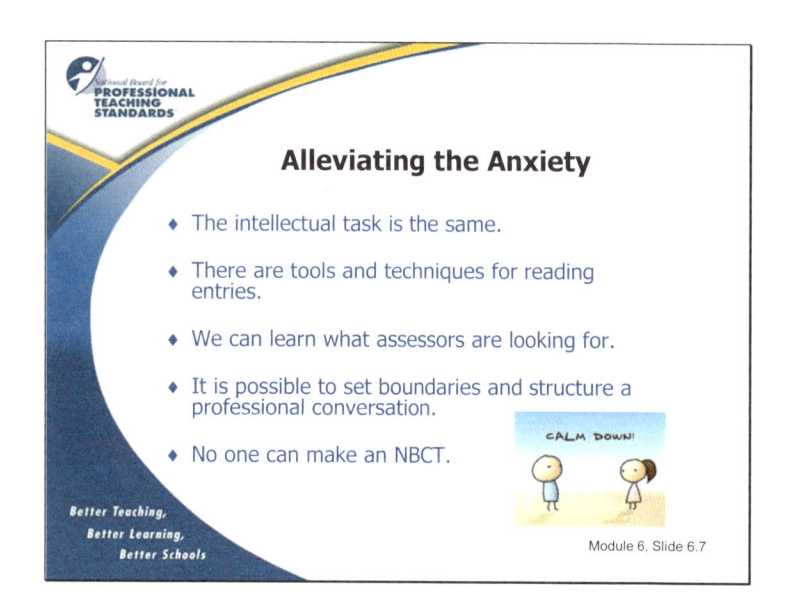

Alleviating the Anxiety

- The intellectual task is the same.
- There are tools and techniques for reading entries.
- We can learn what assessors are looking for.
- It is possible to set boundaries and structure a professional conversation.
- No one can make an NBCT.

Module 6, Slide 6.7

Notes:

Lesson 2: The Thinking Process

During this lesson, you will:

- Learn about the three different levels of thinking that are required in portfolio entries.
- Practice elevating a candidate's thinking.

Module 6, Slide 6.8

Notes:

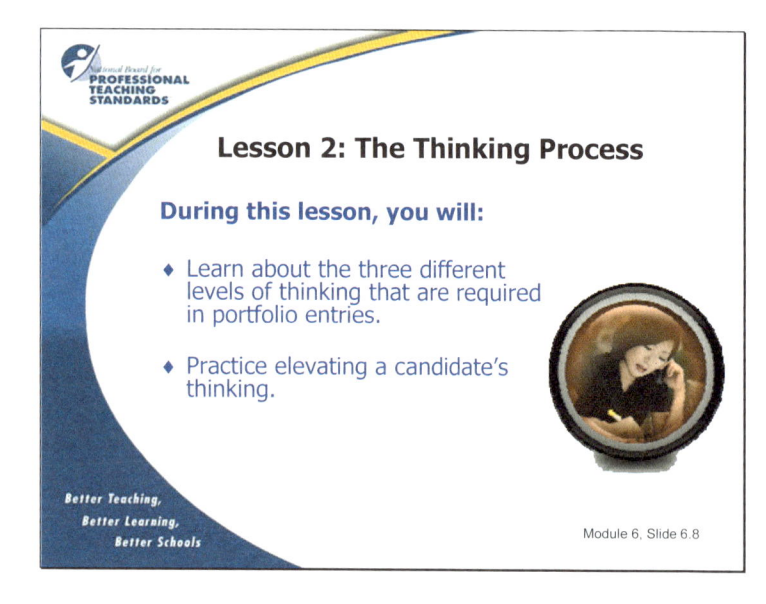

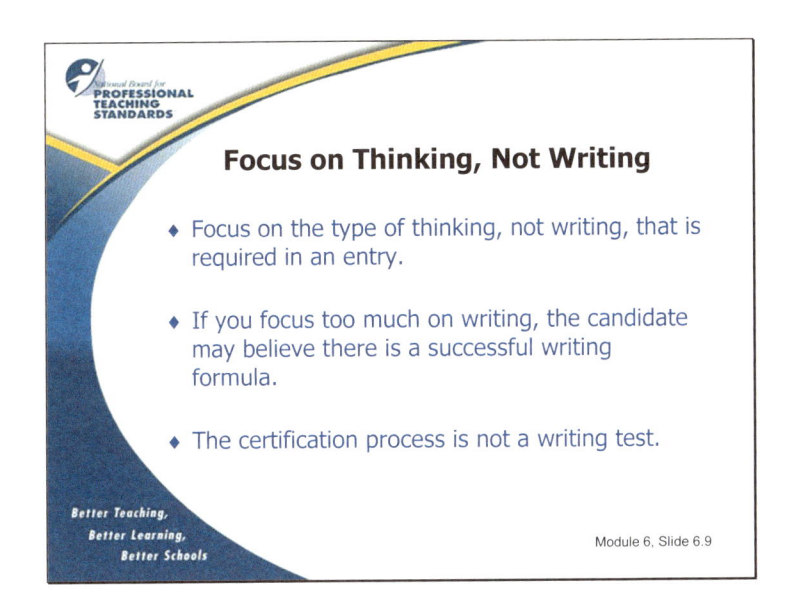

Module Six: Portfolio Entry Review

Focus on Thinking, Not Writing

- Focus on the type of thinking, not writing, that is required in an entry.
- If you focus too much on writing, the candidate may believe there is a successful writing formula.
- The certification process is not a writing test.

Module 6, Slide 6.9

Notes:

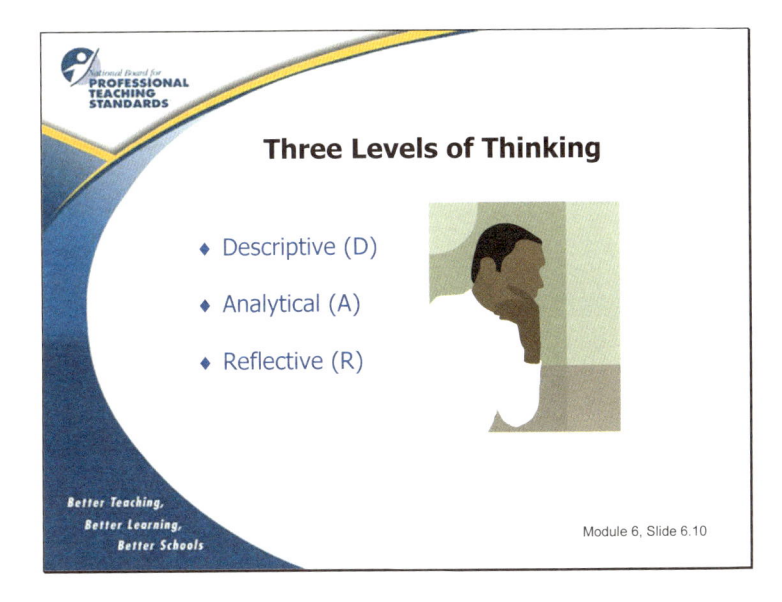

Three Levels of Thinking

- Descriptive (D)
- Analytical (A)
- Reflective (R)

Module 6, Slide 6.10

Notes:

Candidate Support Provider Training

6.7

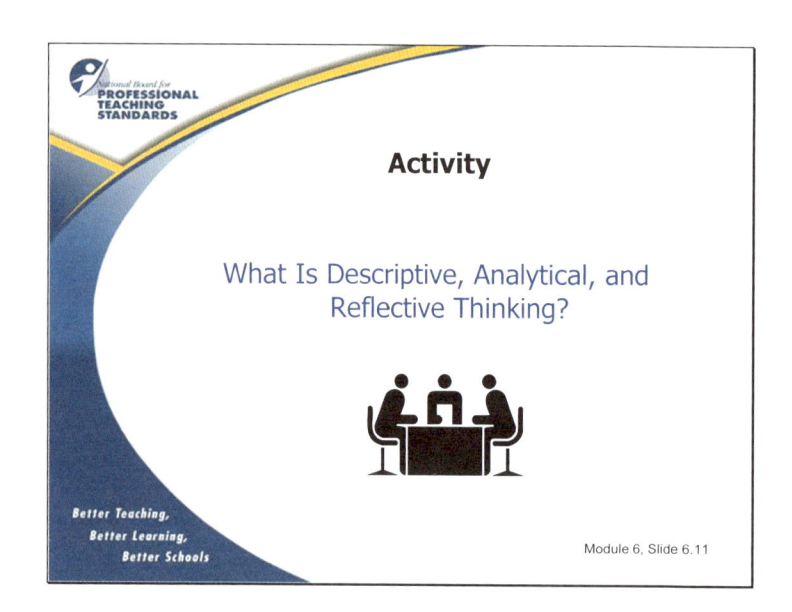

MODULE SIX: PORTFOLIO ENTRY REVIEW

Activity

What Is Descriptive, Analytical, and Reflective Thinking?

Module 6, Slide 6.11

Notes:

Module Six: Portfolio Entry Review

ACTIVITY: WHAT IS DESCRIPTIVE, ANALYTICAL, AND REFLECTIVE THINKING?

PURPOSE:

The purpose of this activity is to define and provide examples of descriptive, analytical, and reflective thinking.

INSTRUCTIONS:

For your assigned type of thinking, work with your group and:

- Provide key words and phrases that help define the meaning of the level of thinking.

- Develop a few question stems for that level of thinking as it might appear in the written commentary.

Record your ideas on your prepared pieces of chart paper.

Take about **10 minutes** to complete this activity.

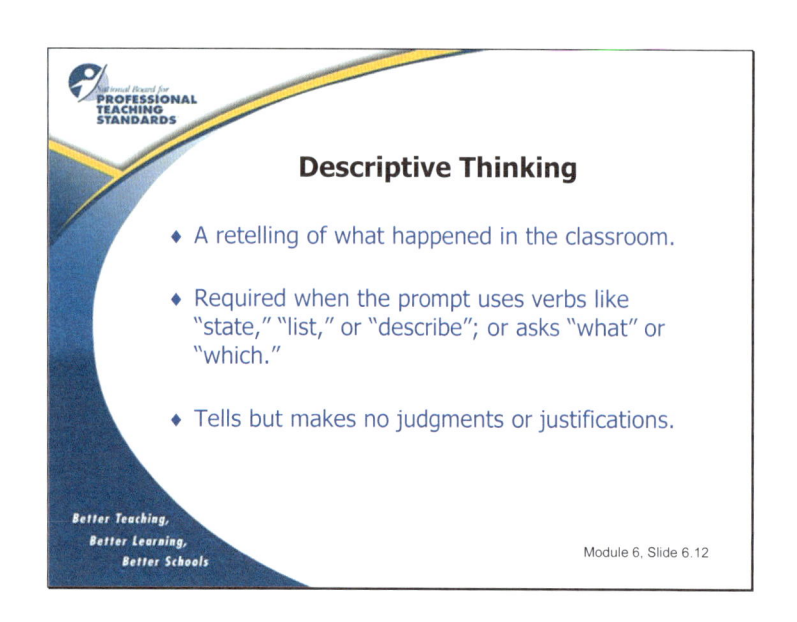

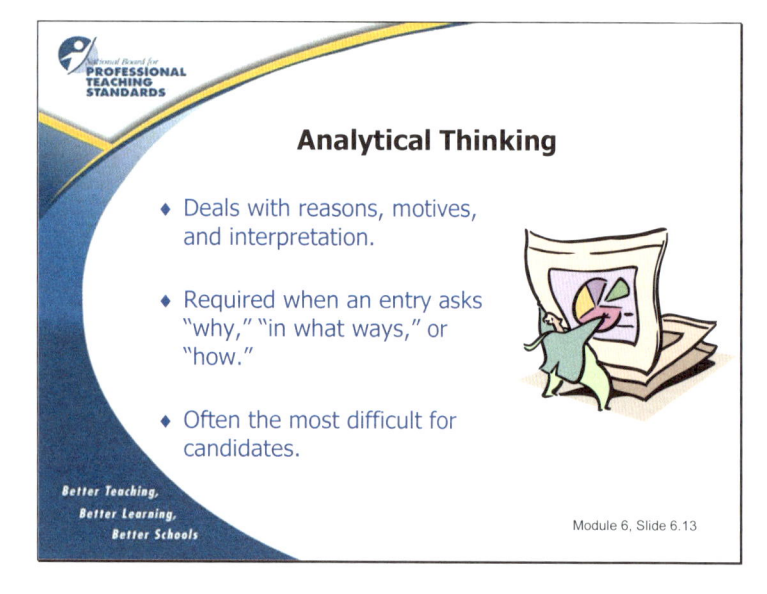

MODULE SIX: PORTFOLIO ENTRY REVIEW

Descriptive Thinking

- A retelling of what happened in the classroom.

- Required when the prompt uses verbs like "state," "list," or "describe"; or asks "what" or "which."

- Tells but makes no judgments or justifications.

Module 6, Slide 6.12

Notes:

Analytical Thinking

- Deals with reasons, motives, and interpretation.

- Required when an entry asks "why," "in what ways," or "how."

- Often the most difficult for candidates.

Module 6, Slide 6.13

Notes:

MODULE SIX: PORTFOLIO ENTRY REVIEW

Reflective Thinking

- The thought process that occurs after teaching.
- Involves contemplating, pondering, evaluating, and planning for the future.
- Required when an entry asks how successful a lesson was, what parts of the lesson candidates would keep the same, and what they would change.

Module 6, Slide 6.14

Notes:

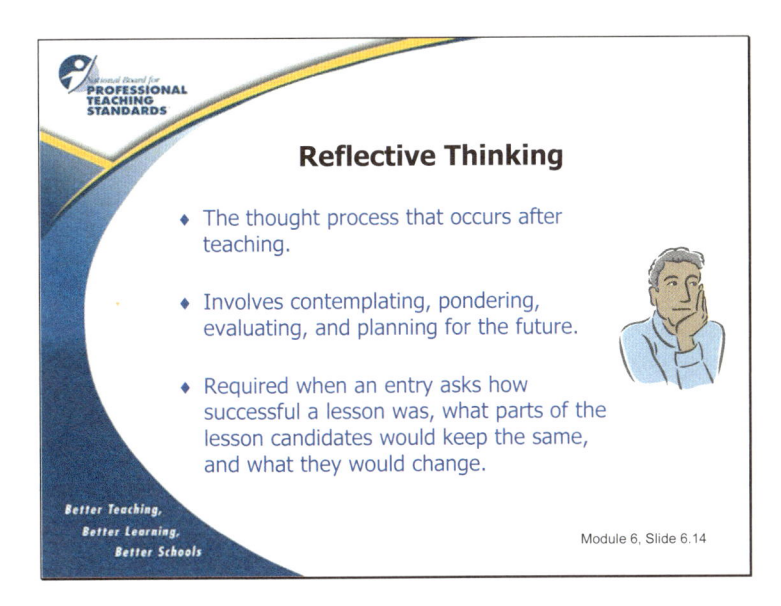

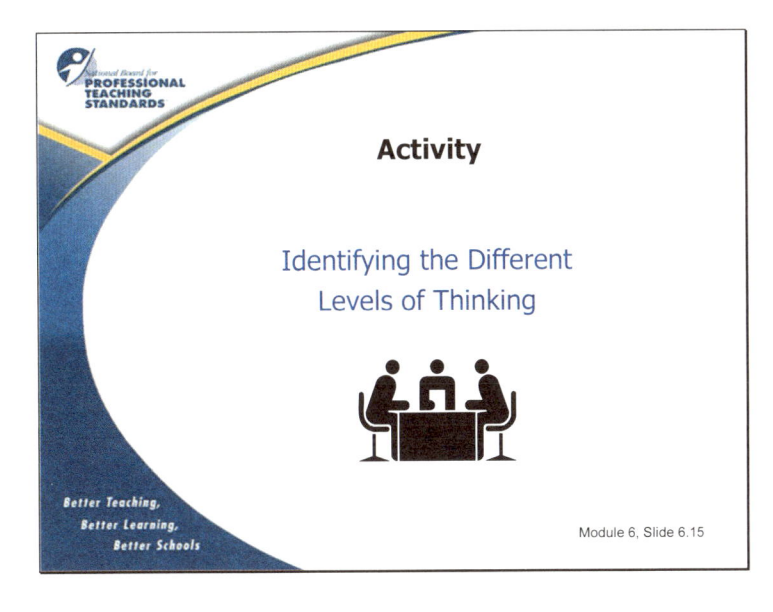

Activity

Identifying the Different Levels of Thinking

Module 6, Slide 6.15

Notes:

MODULE SIX: PORTFOLIO ENTRY REVIEW

ACTIVITY: IDENTIFYING THE DIFFERENT LEVELS OF THINKING

PURPOSE:

The purpose of this activity is to practice identifying the different levels of thinking required in a portfolio entry and to move candidates from the descriptive level of thinking to the analytical and reflective levels.

INSTRUCTIONS:

Pages 1 through 3 in your Portfolio Entry Review Handout contain two candidate attempts at the same entry using the same lesson.

Working individually, read both entry versions and highlight or underline examples of descriptive, analytical, and reflective thinking. Be prepared to share your results with the class.

Take about **15 minutes** to complete this activity.

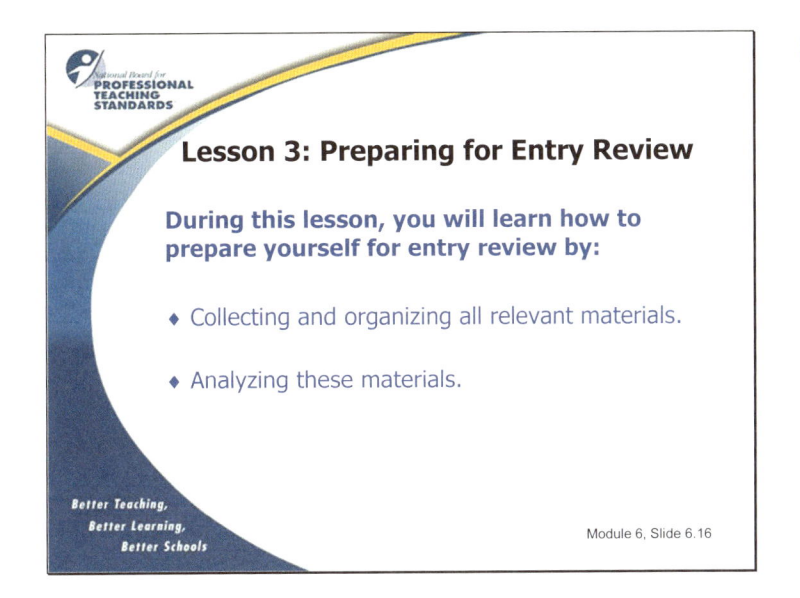

Module Six: Portfolio Entry Review

Lesson 3: Preparing for Entry Review

During this lesson, you will learn how to prepare yourself for entry review by:

- Collecting and organizing all relevant materials.
- Analyzing these materials.

Module 6, Slide 6.16

Notes:

Collect All Materials

Types of documentation:

- The candidate's entry
- Supporting documentation

Module 6, Slide 6.17

Notes:

Candidate Support Provider Training

MODULE SIX: PORTFOLIO ENTRY REVIEW

The Candidate's Entry

Gather the entire entry including:

- Contextual information sheet
- Written commentary
- Student work samples
- Any video recorded requirements

Module 6, Slide 6.18

Notes:

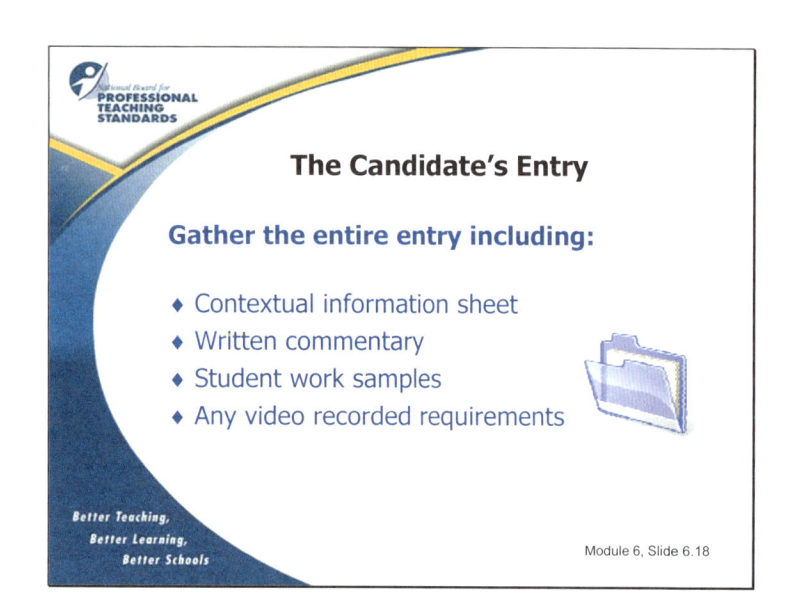

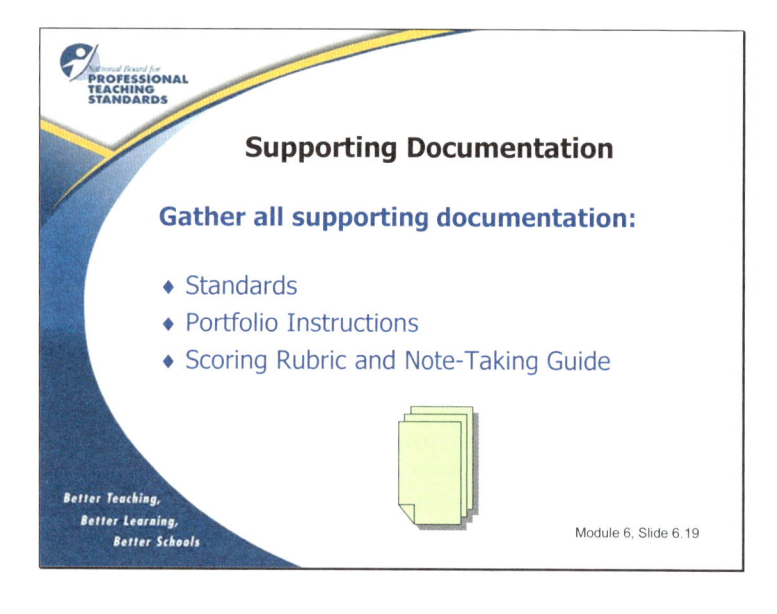

Supporting Documentation

Gather all supporting documentation:

- Standards
- Portfolio Instructions
- Scoring Rubric and Note-Taking Guide

Module 6, Slide 6.19

Notes:

Module Six: Portfolio Entry Review

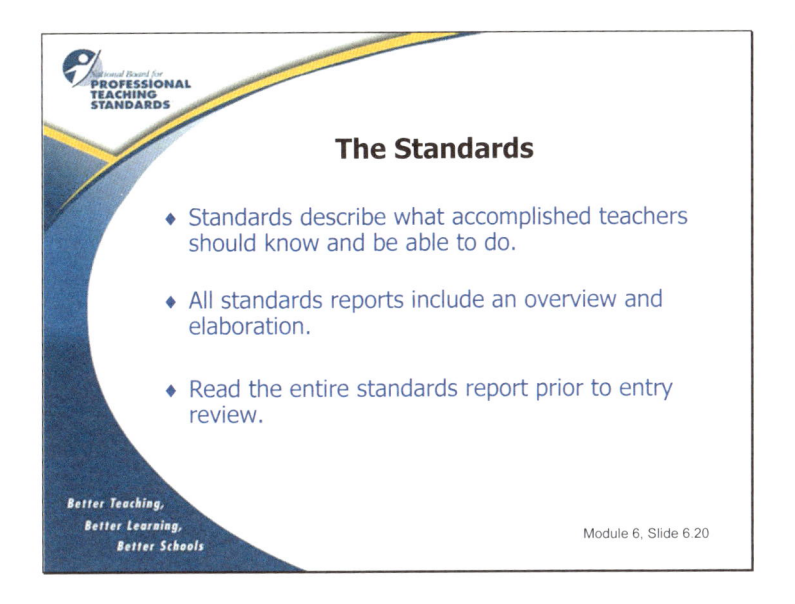

The Standards

- Standards describe what accomplished teachers should know and be able to do.
- All standards reports include an overview and elaboration.
- Read the entire standards report prior to entry review.

Module 6, Slide 6.20

Notes:

Portfolio Instructions

Collect and analyze the following sections:

- Overview and Standards
- What Do I Need to Do?
- How Will My Response Be Scored?
- Composing My Written Commentary
- Making Good Choices

Module 6, Slide 6.21

Notes:

MODULE SIX: PORTFOLIO ENTRY REVIEW

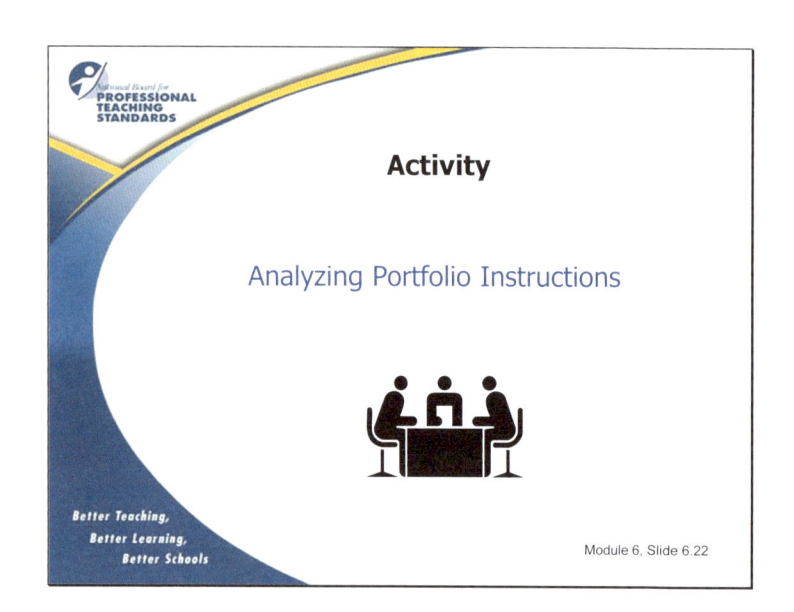

Activity

Analyzing Portfolio Instructions

Module 6, Slide 6.22

Notes:

Module Six: Portfolio Entry Review

ACTIVITY: ANALYZING PORTFOLIO INSTRUCTIONS

PURPOSE:

The purpose of this activity is to practice analyzing an entry's portfolio instructions to become familiar with their overall organization, language, and technical requirements for candidates.

INSTRUCTIONS:

Read your assigned section of the portfolio instructions on **pages 7 through 16** in your Portfolio Entry Review Handout. Then, working with your table group members answer the questions below. Take about **15 minutes** to complete this activity.

1. What specifically does the candidate need to know and be able to do in this entry?

2. What are the technical requirements in this section?

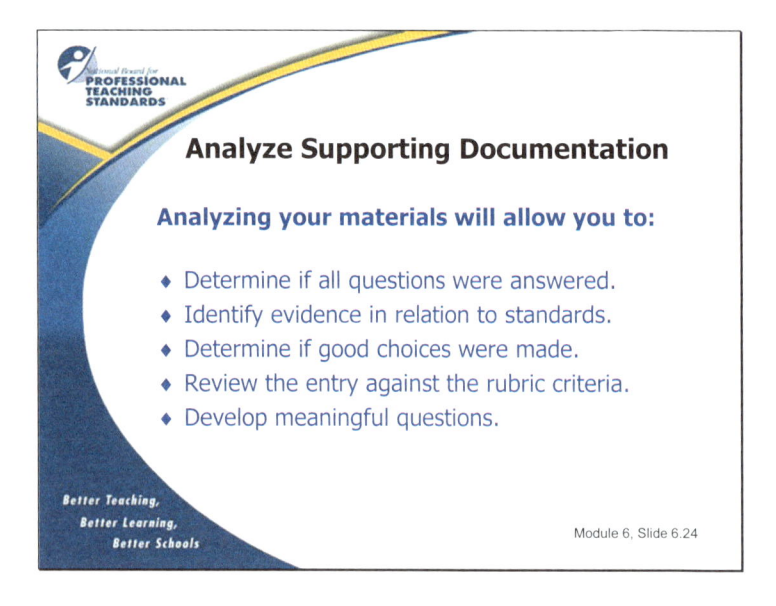

MODULE SIX: PORTFOLIO ENTRY REVIEW

The Scoring Rubric and Note-Taking Guide

- Primarily used by assessors to help them identify and score evidence in an entry.
- The **scoring rubric** describes the characteristics of candidate performance at four major levels of the score scale.
- The **note-taking guide** governs how assessors record the evidence in each entry.

Notes:

Analyze Supporting Documentation

Analyzing your materials will allow you to:

- Determine if all questions were answered.
- Identify evidence in relation to standards.
- Determine if good choices were made.
- Review the entry against the rubric criteria.
- Develop meaningful questions.

Notes:

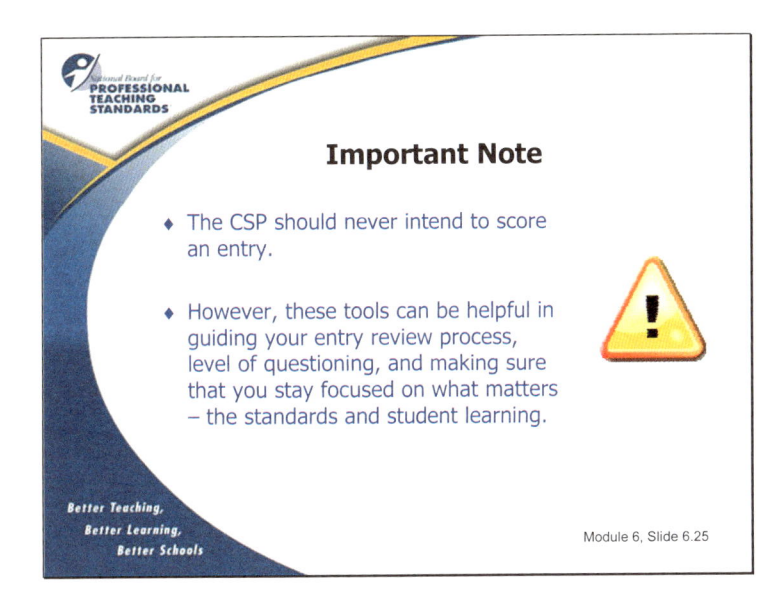

MODULE SIX: PORTFOLIO ENTRY REVIEW

Important Note

- The CSP should never intend to score an entry.

- However, these tools can be helpful in guiding your entry review process, level of questioning, and making sure that you stay focused on what matters – the standards and student learning.

Notes:

Organize All Materials

- Your candidate should gather and organize all materials for you.

- Resist the urge to collect and organize these materials yourself.

- Remember: They need to own the process.

Notes:

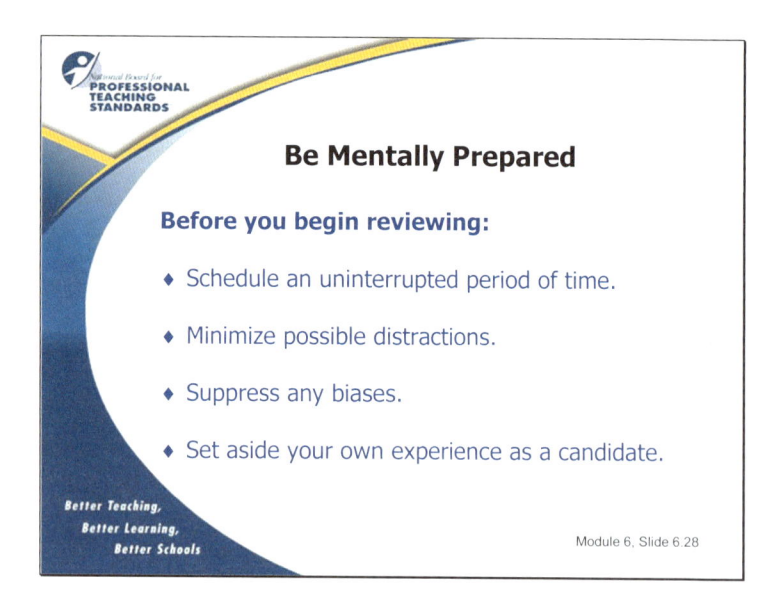

MODULE SIX: PORTFOLIO ENTRY REVIEW

The Folder Method

- **Front:** Overview and Standards
- **Inside Left:** How Will My Entry Be Scored?
- **Inside Right:** Composing My Written Commentary
- **Back:** T-Chart
- Written entry is placed inside.

Module 6, Slide 6.27

Notes:

Be Mentally Prepared

Before you begin reviewing:

- Schedule an uninterrupted period of time.
- Minimize possible distractions.
- Suppress any biases.
- Set aside your own experience as a candidate.

Module 6, Slide 6.28

Notes:

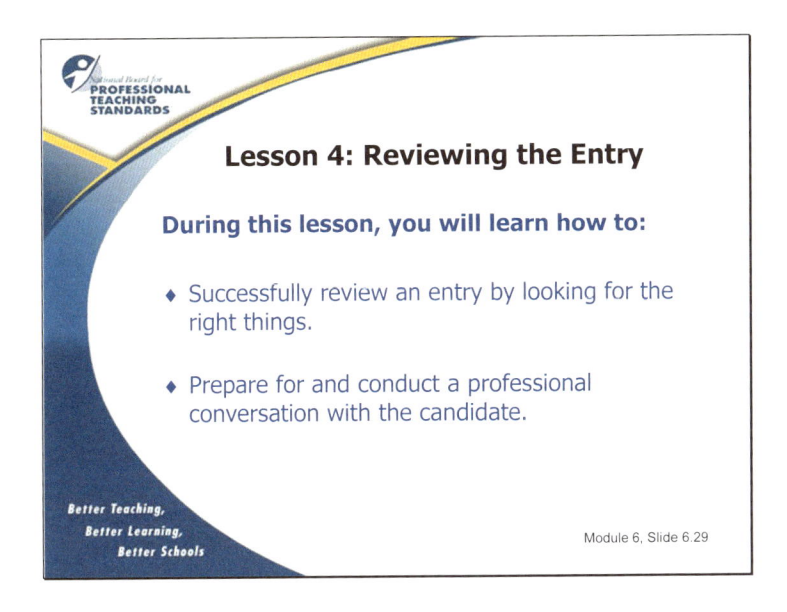

Module Six: Portfolio Entry Review

Lesson 4: Reviewing the Entry

During this lesson, you will learn how to:

- Successfully review an entry by looking for the right things.
- Prepare for and conduct a professional conversation with the candidate.

Module 6, Slide 6.29

Notes:

Three Key Elements in an Entry

1. Answers to all of the **questions**.
2. Clear, consistent, and convincing **evidence** of student learning.
3. Quality of **links** between the evidence.

Module 6, Slide 6.30

Notes:

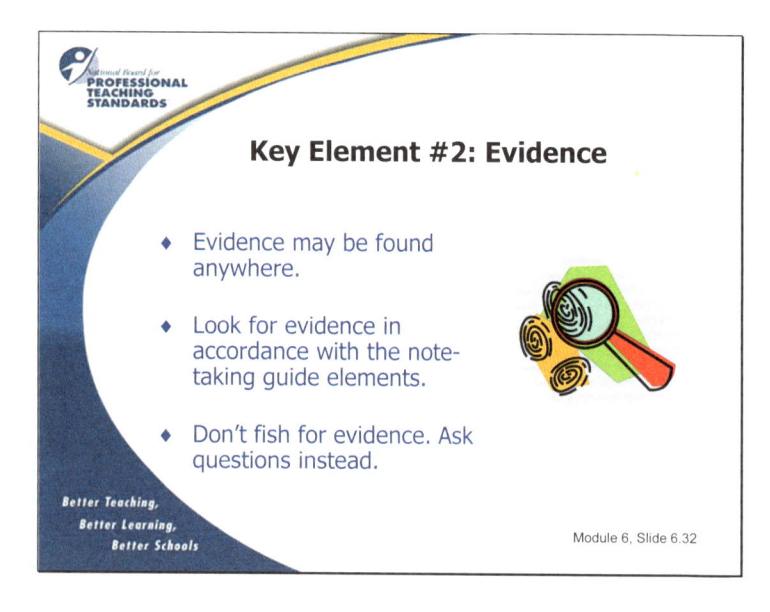

MODULE SIX: PORTFOLIO ENTRY REVIEW

Key Element #1: Questions

- All questions are included in "Composing My Written Commentary."
- Candidates do not have to answer the questions in order.
- If a candidate does not answer a question, this should raise a red flag.

Module 6, Slide 6.31

Notes:

Key Element #2: Evidence

- Evidence may be found anywhere.
- Look for evidence in accordance with the note-taking guide elements.
- Don't fish for evidence. Ask questions instead.

Module 6, Slide 6.32

Notes:

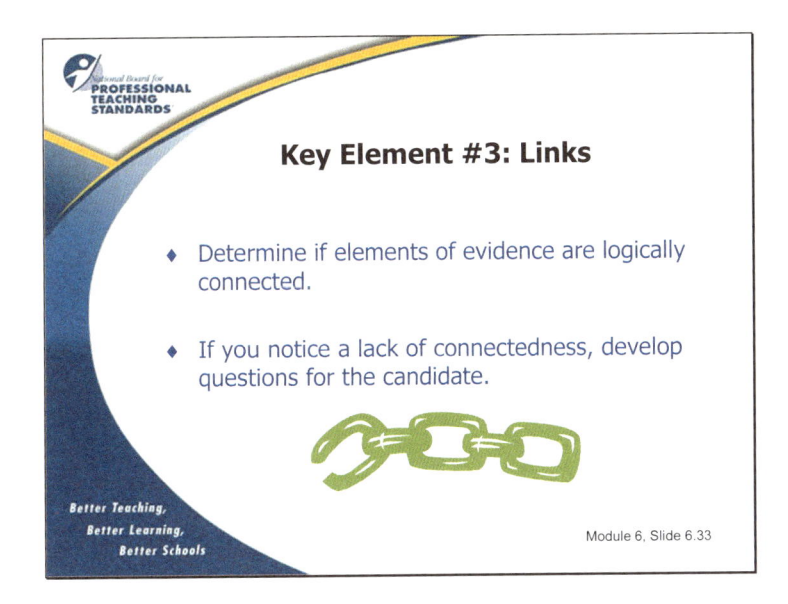

Module Six: Portfolio Entry Review

Key Element #3: Links

- Determine if elements of evidence are logically connected.
- If you notice a lack of connectedness, develop questions for the candidate.

Module 6, Slide 6.33

Notes:

Taking Notes

- Take notes on questions being answered, evidence, and connections between evidence.
- Highlight or underline evidence.
- Develop note-taking tools.

Note: Your notes are for your eyes only.

Module 6, Slide 6.34

Notes:

SAMPLE ENTRY REVIEW NOTE-TAKING CHART

Knowledge of Students (KOS)	Goals/Connections (G/C)
Assignments/Instruction (A/I)	**Content Knowledge/Writing Process (CK/WP)**
Personal Expression (PE)	**Thinking Tool (TT)**
Analysis (Ana)	**Reflection (R)**

Connections:

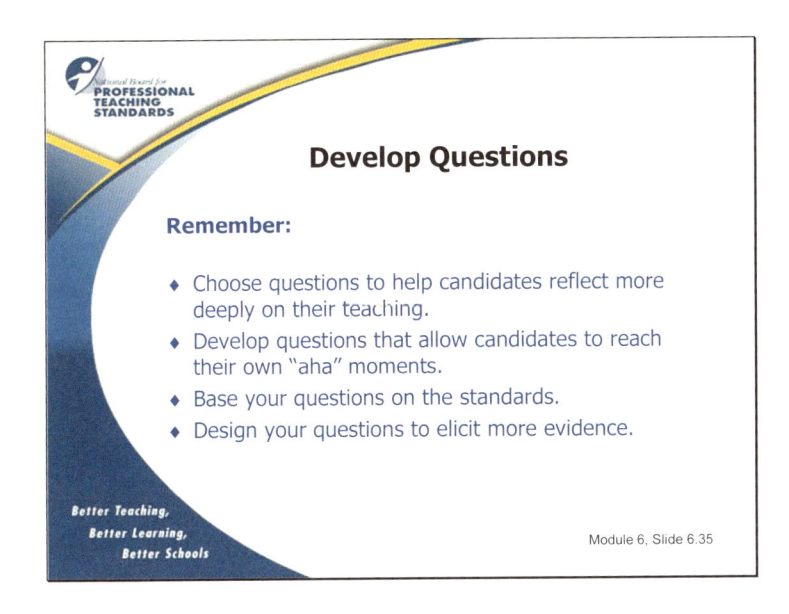

Module Six: Portfolio Entry Review

Develop Questions

Remember:

- Choose questions to help candidates reflect more deeply on their teaching.
- Develop questions that allow candidates to reach their own "aha" moments.
- Base your questions on the standards.
- Design your questions to elicit more evidence.

Module 6, Slide 6.35

Notes:

Have a Professional Conversation

- Providing meaningful feedback without helping the candidate too much is one of the most challenging tasks for CSPs.

- Don't feel frustrated if the first few conversations don't go as smoothly as you'd like.

- This skill takes practice and will develop over time.

Module 6, Slide 6.36

Notes:

MODULE SIX: PORTFOLIO ENTRY REVIEW

Professional Conversation Guidelines

During your professional conversation:

- Keep the principles of adult learning in mind.
- Use core interpersonal skills throughout your meeting.
- Always be respectful of the candidate's practice.
- Set aside your biases.
- Follow the NBPTS ethics guidelines.

Module 6, Slide 6.37

Notes:

Activity

Instructor-Led Entry Review

Module 6, Slide 6.38

Notes:

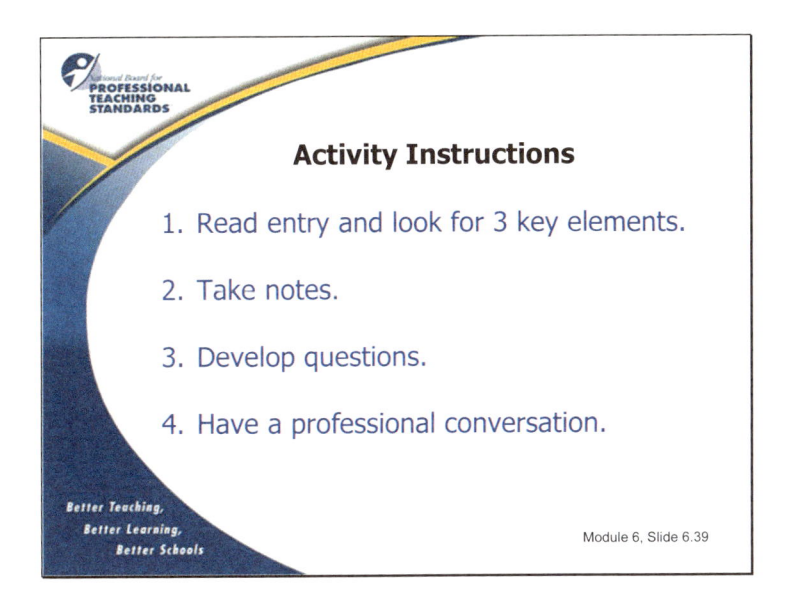

MODULE SIX: PORTFOLIO ENTRY REVIEW

Activity Instructions

1. Read entry and look for 3 key elements.
2. Take notes.
3. Develop questions.
4. Have a professional conversation.

Module 6, Slide 6.39

Notes:

Lesson 5: Practice and Application

During this lesson, you will:

- Individually review an entire portfolio entry.
- Identify 3 key elements—questions, evidence, links.
- Develop effective questions to ask the candidate.

Module 6, Slide 6.40

Notes:

MODULE SIX: PORTFOLIO ENTRY REVIEW

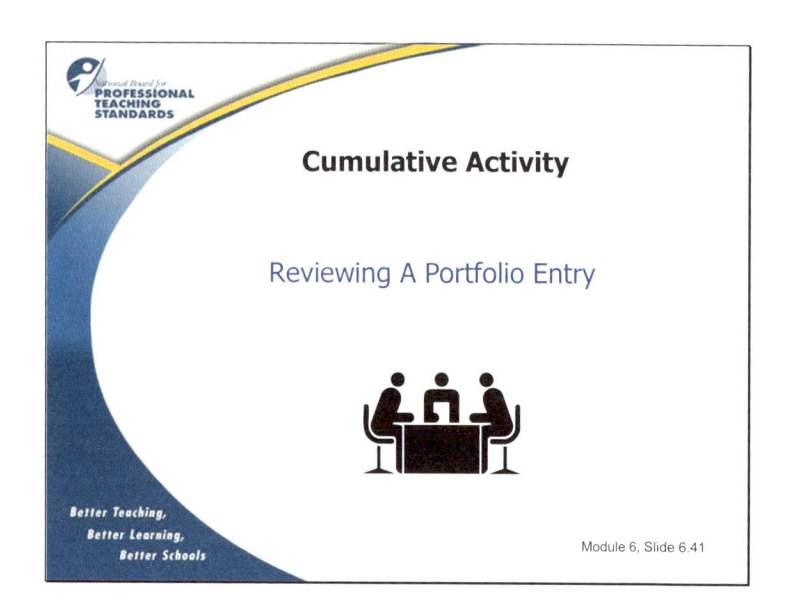

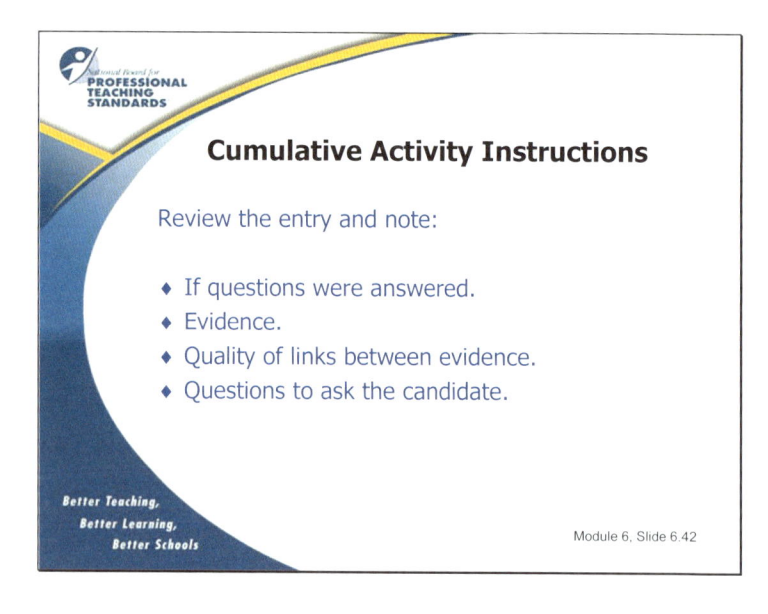

Cumulative Activity

Reviewing A Portfolio Entry

Module 6, Slide 6.41

Notes:

Cumulative Activity Instructions

Review the entry and note:

- If questions were answered.
- Evidence.
- Quality of links between evidence.
- Questions to ask the candidate.

Module 6, Slide 6.42

Notes:

MODULE SIX: PORTFOLIO ENTRY REVIEW

CUMULATIVE ACTIVITY: REVIEWING A PORTFOLIO ENTRY

PURPOSE:

The purpose of this activity is to practice reviewing an entire portfolio entry and taking notes on evidence, connections between the evidence, and questions you can ask the candidate.

INSTRUCTIONS:

Working individually, review the portfolio entry on **pages 29 through 73** in your Portfolio Entry Review Handout. As you review, take notes on the following:

- If all the questions have been addressed.
- Evidence of student learning and standards-based accomplished teaching (Remember to refer back to the elements in the note-taking guide).
- Connections/links between the different pieces of evidence.
- Questions to ask the candidate to deepen his or her thinking.

Feel free to write on the entry and use the note-taking chart on **page 6.24** in your Participant Manual.

Remember: the abbreviated standards, portfolio instructions, scoring rubric, and note-taking guide for this entry are included on **pages 5 through 24** in the Portfolio Entry Review Handout. Your table group has a copy of the full entry standards.

Take about **one hour** to complete his activity.

Module Six Summary

During this module, you learned and practiced:

- The important role of entry reviewers.
- Different levels of thinking required in entries.
- How to prepare for entry review.
- A structured process for reviewing entries.

Notes:

Module Seven:
Summary

Module Seven: Summary

Module Overview

During this final module, you will discuss what parts of training were most effective and in what areas you wish to continue to develop. You will have an opportunity to provide written feedback and comments on the effectiveness of the training.

Learning Objectives

After completing this module you will be able to:

- Identify what parts of training were most helpful to you.
- Identify areas in which you wish to continue to develop.

MODULE SEVEN: SUMMARY

CANDIDATE SUPPORT PROVIDER TRAINING
COURSE EVALUATION FORM

INSTRUCTIONS: Please answer the questions below. Your evaluation data will be used to improve future training deliveries of this course. Once completed, please return this form to the instructor before leaving the classroom. Thank you for participating in the *Candidate Support Provider* training.

1. Please describe your experience as a candidate support provider (if any).

2. Please list any previous training you have received on providing candidate support.

CANDIDATE SUPPORT PROVIDER TRAINING
COURSE EVALUATION FORM (cont'd)

3. Please indicate how knowledgeable you were about each topic **before** taking this course and how knowledgeable you are about each topic **after** taking the course. Assign a rating of 1 to 9 using the scale below. Write your answers in the boxes provided.

```
   1        2        3        4        5        6        7        8        9
No Knowledge                    Moderate Knowledge                Extensive Knowledge
```

TOPIC	BEFORE	AFTER
The National Board Certification Process (applicable if you attended the pre-training session)		
The Architecture of Accomplished Teaching		
The Role and Responsibilities of Candidate Support Providers		
Legal and Ethical Responsibilities of Candidate Support Providers		
NBPTS Scoring Process and Procedures		
Retake Procedures and Support		
Core Interpersonal Communication Skills (Attending, Observing, Listening, Asking Questions, Using Positive Presuppositions)		
Elevating Candidate Thinking Through Effective Questioning		
Examining Bias and Diversity		
The Three levels of Thinking (Descriptive, Analytical, Reflective)		
The Entry Review Process		
Reviewing Portfolio Entries		
Providing Meaningful Feedback to Candidates		

MODULE SEVEN: SUMMARY

**CANDIDATE SUPPORT PROVIDER TRAINING
COURSE EVALUATION FORM (cont'd)**

---

4. What were the **strengths** of the course?

5. What could be done to **improve** the course?

6. Overall, how would you rate the *Candidate Support Provider* course?

1	2	3	4	5	6	7	8	9
Poor				**Good**				**Excellent**

CANDIDATE SUPPORT PROVIDER TRAINING
COURSE EVALUATION FORM (cont'd)

7. Overall, how would you rate the participant materials provided to you? (i.e., Participant Manual, handouts)

   1   2   3   4   5   6   7   8   9
   Poor   **Good**   **Excellent**

8. Overall, how would you rate your instructor(s)?

   1   2   3   4   5   6   7   8   9
   Poor   **Good**   **Excellent**

THANK YOU!

Module Seven: Summary

Notes: